REFLECTIONS IN A LAKE

This book is to be returned on or before
the last date stamped below.

10 F

24.APR.89   1

26.JUN89   16716

29.JAN90 123698

-4 JAN93 5748

15 MAR93 8486

19.APR93 018745

10.MAY93 0194

28. OCT. 1997

2 6 MAR 2010

Reflections in a Lake

A STUDY OF CHEKHOV'S FOUR GREATEST PLAYS

Caryl Brahms

WEIDENFELD AND NICOLSON   LONDON

© Caryl Brahms 1976

Weidenfeld and Nicolson
11 St John's Hill London SW11

ISBN 0 297 77194 9

Setting by
TRI-AM Photoset Ltd
Bridge Foot, Warrington
Printed by Morrison & Gibbs Ltd
London and Edinburgh

to the vivid memory of Nora Nicholson, actress

Contents

Acknowledgements

All quotations from the plays off Chekhov are taken from *Anton Chekhov: Plays* (Penguin Classics, 1959) translated by Elizaveta Fen, copyright © Elizaveta Fen, 1951, 1954, reprinted by permission of Penguin Books Ltd. I am grateful for permission to reproduce them, and also to the following for permission to quote other copyright material: Farrar, Straus & Giroux, Inc., New York, *The Selected Letters of Anton Chekhov*, edited by Lillian Hellman, translated by Sidonie Lederer, copyright © 1955 by Lillian Hellman; The Bodley Head, *Letters of Anton Chekhov*, edited by Simon Karlinsky; Jonathan Cape Ltd, *Letters of Anton Chekhov*, edited by Avraham Yarmolinsky.

I am particularly indebted to Ned Sherrin for his help throughout the book; and to John Curtis and Barbara Gough at my publisher's for their advice and assistance.

C.B.

The photographs between pages 84 and 85 are reproduced by kind permission of the following: Mander and Mitchenson Theatre Collection – nos 4, 6, 8, 9, 10, 11; Novosti Press Agency – nos 1, 2, 5; The Shakespeare Birthplace Trust – no. 13; John Vickers – no. 12.

Chronological table

Life

1860 (January 17) Anton Chekhov born in Taganrog the son of a grocer.

1876 His family move to Moscow after collapse of business. He remains to study, supporting himself as a teacher.

1879 Moves to Moscow after matriculating. Studies medi cine at Moscow University and supports his family by writing for humorous papers.

1884 Qualifies. Begins work as a doctor. Suffers his first haemorrhage.

1886 Begins more serious writing, contributing to Petersburg daily, *Novoye Vemrya*.

1888 Awarded Pushkin Prize.

1889 Elected member of the Society of Lovers of Russian Literature.

1890 Travels through Siberia, India and Ceylon. His health deteriorating.

1891 Makes journey to Western Europe.

1892 Organises relief in famine-stricken area. Moves his family to a farm in the Serpukhov district where he is appointed medical superintendent.

1896 Attacked by a haemorrhage of the lungs.

Works

1880 His first story published. Over the next years he contributes hundreds of stories etc, to various periodicals.

1886 *The Swan Song*, a play in one act, completed.

1889 *The Wood Demon* produced in Moscow.

1895 *The Seagull* completed.

1896 *The Seagull* produced in Petersburg. Is a complete failure.

1897 Active in his district, building schools etc. Taken critically ill, hospitalized and convalesces in the South of France.

1898 Disgusted by anti-Dreyfus campaign. His father dies and he moves his family to the Crimea for the sake of his health. Builds house near Yalta.

1899 Sells the copyright of all his past and future work to the publisher Marx.

1900 Elected member of the Academy of Sciences.

1901 Marries Olga Knipper an actress.

1902 Resigns membership of Academy of Sciences in protest to authorities cancelling Gorky's membership.

1903 State of health gets worse. Elected temporary president of the Society of Russian Literature.

1904 Seriously ill. Travels to German health resort with his wife.

1904 (July 2) Dies at Badenweiler. Buried in the cemetery of the Novodevichiy Monastery in Moscow.

1898 *The Seagull* a tremendous success in Moscow. *Uncle Vanya* produced in the provinces with great success.

1899 *Uncle Vanya* produced in Moscow.

1900 *The Three Sisters* begun.

1901 *The Three Sisters* produced in Moscow.

1903 *The Cherry Orchard* completed.

1904 *The Cherry Orchard* produced in Moscow.

Introduction

Sooner or later, in the foyer, it will come – and any practised Chekhovian can see it coming – usually from a detractor, manoeuvring for an opening to pulverize the faithful. 'Which is your favourite Chekhov play?' And there they are, floating like lost souls, in the air between you: *The Seagull, Uncle Vanya, The Three Sisters* and *The Cherry Orchard*. For these are the plays – the great quartet – most frequently to be seen on the English-speaking stage, the plays I invite the playgoer to ponder with me.

'Did you ever have that feeling that you wanted to go, and yet that you wanted to stay?' Thus Schnozzle Durante unknowingly put into a song the problem that haunts those four plays, and I do not know that anyone has ever stated more lucidly the heavy hand of indecision.

The Seagull, a lakeside play of spring and autumn laden with unrequited love, provides the perfect soil from which agitated changes of mind will grow freely. *Uncle Vanya*, a play about obsession, of its very nature breeds the will to break away and the necessity to remain. (Incidentally why did Chekhov label it *Uncle Vanya* when he could have called it after more dramatic characters? In its first statement, a sprawling and wasteful affair, it was called *The Wood Demon*, and not the least significant of the many titles he might have used, *Autumn Roses*, suggests itself. But possibly the title chosen by Chekhov enshrines the universal love for the fool of the family, in the sense of the misfit.)

Events are the causes of much mind-searching among the three sisters who will never get to Moscow and, one shrewdly suspects, would loathe it if they did, on the principle of the summer holiday song:

> Never go back to wherever it was,
> Wherever it was will have changed.

The Cherry Orchard, glimpsed in a Russian Maytime – three degrees of morning frost and the cherry trees launching their blossom on the sighs of their own elegy – depends for its plot on the eternal need to go, and the lassitude of remaining.

We who drift in our own world of bombs and bombast, of strikes and power groups, of white skins and those with a degree of copper in their bronze, drifting, too, in a civilization that stands on the sidelines watching all kinds of horror, including the Irish war of intolerance in which Christian ambushes Christian, we know well why gentle Chekhov was warning the shiftless, love-sapped society in those plays which are the microcosm of middle-class Russia. Gentle Chekhov? Savage, ironic, exasperated, laughing Chekhov. He sang the shabby-genteel theme of the middle-of-the-road Russian apathy and he saw these dream-soaked and for the most part reflective creatures as philosophizing ostriches head-down in a desert of shifting sands; and as he laughed at them he fumed. But since to understand is to forgive, as he fumed he smiled, and his smile was not without tenderness, for it was that of a father with a feckless family of unhappy-go-lucky children who, it was all Lombard Street to a china orange (what am I wagering? – all the Nevsky Prospeckt to the love of three oranges), would be too full of their own problems and obsessions to listen to his.

William Gerhardi, who has written an indispensable book on Chekhov (*Anton Chekhov: A Critical Study*, 1923), is reported to have said: 'In *Vanya*, Astrov talks about the future in a nostalgic way.' A rereading of the text suggests that it was the way of the pre-revolutionary Russian intelligentsia, who were willing to mark the small beginnings of the wind, the merest breeze of change, in the lull before the storm, so long as they were not called on to do anything about it – least of all to weather it: 'The people who come a hundred years or a couple of hundred years after us and despise us for having lived in so stupid and tasteless a fashion – perhaps they'll find a way to be happy. As for us – there's only one hope for you and me . . . the hope that when we're at rest in our graves we may see visions – perhaps even pleasant ones.'

If I were only to see one more play by Chekhov and I were to be given the choice, which would it be? For me, and for a long time, it lay between *The Cherry Orchard*, with its elegiac comment on a passing society from Gaev: – 'Ladies and gentlemen, the sun has set – and *The Three Sisters*.' For a time I was suspended between Lila Kedrova's entirely believable amorous baby of a Ranyevskaia and Marie Tomasova's bitterly bored Masha, who, of the three initially cheerful but ultimately desolate sisters, most makes her tears my own.

Now I know that were I able to see only one last play by Chekhov, though I might find myself torn by a scene here, a speech there – and perhaps particularly by Sonia's last, most moving speech to Vanya: 'We shall hear the angels, we shall see all the heavens covered with stars like diamonds, we shall see all earthly evil, all our sufferings swept away by the grace which will fill the whole world, and our life will become peaceful, gentle, and sweet as a caress . . .' – in the end it would be the Czech Krejca's production for the Theatre Beyond the Gate, with Tomasova's Masha trying to bear the brave music of the band as the soldiers march away from the provincial town in which the lines of her life are set, and with the soldiers, Lieutenant-Colonel Vershinin, the true love of her life.

Krejca's production, finally forbidden by the Czech regime, acted in a language I do not understand, held up to the looking-glass each mood, each rapture and each tragedy. That is, until some other mounting of some other Chekhov play stays time for me with some other players of feeling and the necessary sense of tender fun and gentle tragedy.

One of the abiding miracles of Chekhov's characters is that one can place them. Almost with their first speech they stand revealed to us. We know at once what kind of a man, a woman, a girl they are. Distinct and true as his characterization is, each play has a message – the same message – for his times, as urgent as any that John Arden, John Osborne or Peter Nichols addressed to us: a message which is spoken by the character he has built to deliver it, and within the terms of that character. (In this he is in direct contradiction with Shaw, who, equally didactic, produces his argument from any character to hand.) One cannot doubt, for all the humour and affection in the manner in which Chekhov communicated it, he felt passionately the need to deliver it to us in every major play he wrote. It is, strangely enough, the same message – though with political overtones – that the English poet Arthur Hugh Clough delivered to his Victorian readers, more crystallized in the poem, but less poignant than in Chekhov's speech.

> Say not the struggle nought availeth
> The labour and the wounds are vain

The poem ends:

> And not by Eastern windows only
> When daylight comes, comes in the light,
> In front the sun climbs slow – how slowly,
> But Westward, look, the sun is bright.

Chekhov's message, delivered in an ancient graveyard by an eternal student, thus: 'The moon is rising. [*a pause*] Here is happiness – here it comes! It is coming nearer and nearer; already I can hear its footsteps. And if we never see it – if we may never know it – what does it matter? Others will see it after us.' To us, drifting in our own wind of change – and a very shrill, vociferous east wind it is – Chekhov is a gentle prophet. To the placid society of his own times his was the voice in the wilderness speaking of doom.

Thus in *The Three Sisters*, with the brave martial music fading away, Olga, poor winged bird, says: 'The years will pass, and we shall all be gone for good and quite forgotten. – Our faces and our voices will be forgotten and people won't even know that there were once three of us here. – But our sufferings may mean happiness for the people who come after us. – There'll be a time when peace and happiness reign in the world ...' And Chekhov's audiences knew that in these veiled terms he was pointing to the dreaded revolution.

He held up his plays to them and forced the unwilling Russian society to look into his mirror of truth. And we in our time know that there was writing on the wall.

As the years passed and the British began to know their Chekhov they took him to their hearts. Though not every serious playgoer would agree with me that his plays come second only to those of Shakespeare in understanding the human heart, and second to none in forgiveness of its weaknesses, most of them might admit that of his four major plays, three and threequarters are masterpieces. If I rate *The Seagull* as something short of perfect it is not because it shows any less understanding of man's behaviour, but that, like Ibsen's *Hedda Gabler*, its end is so abrupt that one finds oneself making free with Judge Brack's final half-stunned protest: 'But plays don't end like this!'

The British, in their productions, have moved in on Chekhov. They have hung his drawing-rooms with their own decently faded chintzes. They have peopled his decaying estates with Aunt Lillians and Uncle Andrews. They see the ladies and gentlemen of the Russian provinces at the turn of the century as feckless and polite – and they may well be right – and the peasants as quaint as those toy-shop Russian families: brightly painted papoushkas and mamoushkas complete with facsimiles in dwindling scale, which fit neatly inside the prototypes in the nurseries of the nicer kind of child. And as to Moscow, Harkov, St Petersburg, why, are they not quite simply Maidstone, Cheltenham, Edinburgh? Indeed when the Moscow Art Theatre plays Chekhov we half resent it. They all seem so ordinary – so vulgar – without Dame Edith or Sir John.

Yet as time has passed, presenting us with more and more problems which we have been unable to solve, torrents which we have been unable to stem, forebodings which we have been unwilling to face, a strange transition seems to have taken place. Can it be that Liubov Ranyevskaia has not, after all, become Aunt Lillian but rather that Aunt Lillian is Liubov Ranyevskaia under the skin?

That irreverent humorist S. J. Simon, with whom I used to write until he died, born in Vladivostock (one-up-manship when all I could produce on my side was Surrey) of Russian parents but educated at an English public school and living in London, used to say that going to a play by Chekhov should be like going to the ballet or the opera, only funnier if possible, which he doubted. One should always be seeing the play for about the fourth time, he held, comparing performances, relishing different interpretations. Certainly one should always be going home to the cherry orchard before the axe falls, or dropping in on three sisters next door, who imagine, poor darlings, that in Moscow tomorrow will be different. Thinking leniently, too, of Uncle Gaev endlessly addressing the bookcase. Uncle Gaev who so gently speaks the epithet of the leisured society of Russia: 'The sun's gone down, ladies and gentlemen', or in the more poetic translation, 'The sun has set, dear friends.' Of Uncle Vanya, too, arriving with his pathetic bunch of autumn roses for the lady in the other man's arms. Of schoolmaster Koolyghin bobbing up in his red crêpe beard to distract his wife who is weeping for his rival. Life is like that. And Chekhov laughs, forgivingly and lovingly, at the lot of us. He is the father of our family and the laughter, the nostalgia and tenderness are called out by family jokes: 'Do you remember when Uncle Vanya tried to shoot the professor and missed him – twice?' 'If you cry "Forward" you must without fail explain in which direction' (this was among some fragments found after his death).

These and their kind are the jokes of the Family Chekhov.

'I have finished *The Cherry Orchard*,' he wrote to a friend, of the last of the great quartet of pieces on a single theme, 'but it is not a drama after all. More of a comedy, even a farce.' A farce on the theme: 'The Day of Judgement is at hand'.

'Ten or fifteen years ago,' the provincial actress Arkadina remarks in *The Seagull* to the popular author she trails round like a frond of seaweed, 'you could always hear music and singing on this lake – almost every night. There are six country houses around the lake. I remember such laughter, and noise, and shooting – love affairs, love affairs all the time.' And at the end of the scene, Dorn, the doctor who is full of years, says: 'How distraught they all are! How distraught! And what a quantity of love about!'

Love, tears, laughter and introspection: these form the *fugato* of a Chekhovian play. With him as with Turgenev, 'Desolation is a delicate thing.' He is said to be the dramatist of farewells, for his plays take place between arrivals and departures. We feel for the people in the plays because they feel for one another, yet they are as powerless to help one another as we, who watch, are powerless to help them – or ourselves for that matter. His plays are filled with love and dejection, hope and despair – hope, that is, for the kind of people who are to come; despair for the people in the Chekhovian present. They are passages in a piece of music, written now with the fun of Mozart, now with the nostalgia of Stravinsky. The themes of love, hope, despair weave in and out of the patterns of sound until we see the whole of a doomed society, of which they are the symbol; hear their pleas for our forgiveness in the broken sentences which will never be finished; watch them moving nearer and nearer to the rim of the abyss; doomed yet finding consolation in the sure knowledge that though it will not be for them that the trumpets sound on the other side, yet will they ring out clarion clear, heralding a new society.

Does hindsight matter – save to the historian? Now that we know that the moon is just a dark scrabble of burnt-out earth, what is the point of getting to Moscow? Far better to go to a theatre where we will be giving one of the four great plays of Chekhov, in our British way, no doubt, but raptly.

The Seagull

Melikhovo, October 21, 1895

. . . I am writing a play which, probably, I also shall finish no earlier than toward the end of November . . . four acts; a landscape (view of a lake); lots of literary talk, little action, a ton of love . . .

Since the play was *The Seagull*, this, the first intimation of immortality though not in precisely the sense Wordsworth indicated – 'Heaven lies about us in our infancy' – at least contained to a certain extent tidings of joy; 'I am writing it not without enjoyment, even though I am frightfully unfaithful to stage conventions.'

That the labour had begun was imparted in this letter to A. S. Suvorin, yet it took second place to other news: 'First of all, this spring I shall be building a new school in the village.' He had opened with this as an excuse for not going to St Petersburg, which Suvorin had been pressing on him, and the argument for and against continued in a second letter, this time from Moscow:

Moscow, October 26, 1895

. . . No, do not tempt me needlessly. I cannot come before November. I shall not leave until I finish the play. And having arrived, I shall stop not with you [the letter continued implacably], but at the France on Bolshaya Morskaya, for I have work up to my ears, if I stayed with you I should walk about and look for someone to chat with, and in a week, no more, I should start chasing myself out of Petersburg, frightened by my idleness. I intend to stay in Petersburg no less than a month.

And back in Melikhovo he wrote:

Melikhovo, November 10, 1895

. . . My play is moving ahead; for the time being everything is going swimmingly, but what may befall later on, toward the end, I know not. Shall finish [Oh rash dramatist!] in November.

The Moscow Imperial Theatre had promised him an advance 'if the play is found suitable'. The letter concluded characteristically: 'It must be because of the play that my pulse is more frequently intermittent, I fall asleep at a late hour and, in general, feel wretched, although since my return from Moscow I have been leading a life of moderation in all respects. I ought to go in for sea-bathing and get me a wife.'

Eleven days later, good news came from Melikhovo:

Melikhovo, November 21, 1895

. . . Well, sir, I have finished my play. I began it *forte* and wound it up *pianissimo* [The present writer would have said it began with a whimper and ended with a bang – from Konstantin's gun] contrary to all the precepts of dramatic art. The end product was a novella.

Chekhov, authorlike, was to find that between the vision and the achievement lies a cooling off. 'I am more dissatisfied than satisfied,' he recorded, 'and, while reading my new-born play I became convinced once more that I am no dramatist.' His saving conviction, however, was that he had written only the skeleton of his piece and that it had yet to be fleshed out with 'a million changes'.

'And what a quantity of love about! – It's the magic lake!' says Dorn the doctor, voicing one aspect of Chekhov's *Seagull* – the love that draws Konstantin and Nina on to their catastrophe; the lake from which no one in the play can ever wholly escape; the sorcery that brings them all back to its glassy calm. 'I am drawn to this place, to this lake, as if I were a seagull,' says the young Nina, speaking more truly than she realizes.

The play, compelling and highly charged with conflicting emotions, has the advantage of beginning with what are probably the two best-known opening lines in the history of the theatre. 'Why,' asks the schoolmaster of Masha, one of the play's minor characters, 'do you always wear black?' The wayward young woman answers, 'I am in mourning for my life.'

Now I think there can be little doubt that Chekhov's contemporary audiences would have smiled at that line, and this settles for me, at least, the old question of whether the British are wrong to play the touching plays of the Chekhovian canon as tragedy, when the Russians play them as comedy. Max Wall, the stand-up music-hall comedian of our own times, has inherited one of his most endearing gags from this source: 'I'm wearing black,' he observes dolefully. 'I am in mourning for my material.' As Stanislavski wrote: 'You will notice that Chekhov's plays are accompanied by the continuous laughter of the audience, which never rings so often and so loud and so clear as it does in his plays . . .' Chekhov wrote, on the whole, with irony about the human condition – an irony based on observation and softened by understanding and pity. He defined bourgeois society just as his audience lived it, and warned – always he warned – of the holocaust to come. It is we, the cool British audience, who are nostalgic as we watch lovers and idlers, gamblers and eternal scholars, mellowed age and crabbed youth, sounding their jangled chimes through the plays.

Audiences, then, in Britain, view the small bunch of immortal and, for their times, tough plays, through a veil, wistfully. Fortunately actors and actresses are quick to sense a laugh – or should be – and while we in the auditorium sit and sigh, get on with the business of laughter-making – laughter, the great collaboration between actor and audience, which does not necessarily come in the same place twice, but surprises us perpetually as audiences change.

What, more precisely, is *The Seagull* about? As Desmond MacCarthy, that critic with the enviable insight, wrote: 'It is a beautiful study in human nature, penetrating and compassionate. In the course of an hour or two we get to know a group of people very well ... somewhere the river of life is rushing sparkling by while each one feels himself or herself stagnating in a backwater.'

Chekhov meant us to be quite clear about the string of events on which he has strung his main plot. Trigorin, 'popular' writer ('if you've been reading Tolstoy, or Zola, you don't feel like reading Trigorin afterwards'), the agent of destruction, gives us the overall plot in a sentence: ' ... a young girl, like you, has lived beside a lake from childhood,' he tells Nina. 'She loves the lake as a seagull does, and she's happy and free as a seagull. But a man chances to come along, sees her, and having nothing better to do, destroys her, just like this seagull here' – and he indicates the dead bird. But, as always with Chekhov's four greatest plays, there is more than one plot weaving and interweaving through the acts. Let the characters unfold some of the themes as they introduce themselves.

We will start with Arkadina, an ageing actress. 'I remember ever so long ago, when you were still playing in the state-aided theatres,' her son begins an anecdote (I prefer the translation 'Imperial Theatre'), and that word 'still' is a key that unlocks Arkadina's character. There is little left in her, now, but the airs and graces of a flamboyant touring actress ('Oh, what could be more boring than this cloying country boredom! . . . Nobody doing anything, everybody talking like a philosopher. – It's nice to be here with you, my friends, it's pleasant to listen to you, – how much better to be sitting alone but in a hotel room learning a part!'); her parsimony (asked to buy a suit for her son, she says, 'I have no money! I'm an actress . . .' and again, 'Well, I do have some money, but after all I'm an actress: my dress-bill alone is enough to ruin me'); the ebb and flow of her affection for a tiresome son she does not understand (in one of many outbursts she cries, 'You're incapable of writing even a couple of miserable scenes! You're just a little upstart from Kiev! A cadger!' Her son replies, 'You miser!' She screams, 'You beggar!'); her passion for the writer Trigorin, many years her junior (she puts her arms round Trigorin and kisses him. 'My beautiful, my wonderful – You the last page of my life! [*Kneels before him.*] 'My joy, my pride, my happiness – [*Embraces his knees.*] If you leave me even for a single hour I shall never survive it, I shall go out of my mind – my wonderful, magnificent man, my master . . .').

Konstantin is in love with Nina, the daughter of a disapproving neighbour. 'A young man, intelligent, living in the country,' says Sorin, trying to explain her son to Arkadina, 'with no money, no position, no future . . . Ashamed and afraid of his idleness . . . he does feel in a way that he doesn't belong here, that he's a cadger, living on charity. It's not to be wondered at – he's got pride.'

Konstantin comes in carrying a seagull he has wantonly shot. He and Nina are by the lakeside, alone. 'I was despicable enough to kill this seagull today. I'm laying it at your feet. Soon I shall kill myself in the same way.' He is a writer – 'We need new art forms!' – indeed a good writer in the making. Yet he would give anything for the novelist Trigorin's flashier, more meretricious, gift: 'He would just mention the neck of a broken bottle glistening on the dam and the black shadow of a mill-wheel – and there you'd have a moonlit night.'

MacCarthy has something to add at this point: 'I often say to myself that a work of art to have any value must have within it the suggestion of valuable life. [A premise that, with the depths of Russian literature staring us in the face, is hard to prove.] Where is that suggestion here? The answer is in the mind of Chekhov himself: in the infection we catch from the spirit of the whole play; in the delicate, truthful, humorous, compassionate mind which observed, understood and forgave.'

Konstantin writes a play for one character, Nina, with a monologue John Arden might well have written today, beginning: 'The men, the lions, the eagles, the partridges, the antlered deer, the geese, the spiders, the silent fishes of the deep, starfishes and creatures unseen to the eye – in short, all living things, all living things, having completed their mournful cycle, have been snuffed out.' It may seem a little strange, at first sight, that Chekhov should have written a monologue so profound and, in its own way poignant, to indicate the fledgling dramatist's present achievement ('We need new art forms!') and promise for the future. But Chekhov's characters, closely though he scanned them, were rarely absent from the light of his own humour, even at their most tragic, and the monologue captures in one deft stroke the talent of the young dramatist – a talent that must inevitably overreach itself – and the company's amusement as the edifice, erected to impress his mother, trembles on the brink.

Konstantin discovers that Nina does not love him: 'You look at me coldly, my presence seems to embarrass you ... Your growing coldness towards me is frightening, it's incredible! – It is as if I woke one day and saw this lake suddenly drying up, or draining away into the ground.' The lake – always the lake, until it seems to be a character in its own right, its reflecting and irresistible right. 'Ten or fifteen years ago you could always hear music and singing on this lake – almost every night,' Arkadina recalls; 'remember such laughter, and noise, and shooting – and love affairs, love affairs all the time.' And Nina says to Trigorin: 'Do you see a house with a garden on the other side?' [of the lake] 'I was born there. I've spent all my life beside this lake and I know every tiny island on it.'

Nina falls in love with Trigorin, Arkadina's lover. She sends him a note with a quotation from one of his own romantic novels: 'If ever you need my life, come and take it.' This is precisely what Trigorin does. When he has tired of the young girl and her simplicities he abandons her to drift back to the lake. Towards the end of the play, Nina, by now a provincial touring actress, pale with hunger and fatigue and raddled with the tawdry experiences of her kind, comes out of a storm one night, and speaks to Konstantin of her life with Trigorin:

NINA: Yesterday, late in the evening I came into the garden to see whether our stage was still there. And it is still standing! I began to cry for the first time in two years, and it lifted the weight from my heart ... Have I changed a lot?

TREPLIOV: ... You are thinner and your eyes have grown bigger. Nina ...

NINA: ... I am so tired. Oh, I wish I could rest – just rest! I'm a seagull. – No, that's not it. I'm an actress ... He didn't believe in the theatre, he was always laughing at my dreams, and so gradually I ceased to believe, too ... And then I was so preoccupied with love and jealousy, and a constant fear for my baby – I became petty and common, when I acted I did it stupidly.

The Konstantin–Nina theme is very much a reflection, as it were in the lake, of Chekhov's own early life and first love.

As for Trigorin, the writer who is seedy in his soul, a kind of walking notebook – indeed he is scribbling a note about Masha: when first we meet him: 'Takes snuff and drinks vodka. Always dresses in black. A schoolmaster in love with her' – is there not, even in this shoddy character, more than a touch of Chekhov himself?

TRIGORIN: ... You know what it is to have a *fixed idea*, for instance when a man keeps on thinking about the same thing day and night, about – let us say, the moon. Well, I, too, have a kind of moon of my own. I'm obsessed day and night by one thought: I must write, I must write, I just must. – For some reason, as soon as I've finished one novel, I feel I must start writing another, then another, then another. – I write in a rush, without stopping, and can't do anything else. What is there radiant or beautiful in that, I ask you? Oh, it's a fatuous life! Here I am with you, I'm quite worked up, and yet not for a single moment do I forget that there's an unfinished novel waiting for me. I look over there and I see a cloud shaped like a grand piano. – At once I think I must put it into some story or other – the fact that a cloud looking like a grand piano has floated by. There's the scent of heliotrope in the air. I make a mental note: 'sickly scent – flower – the colour of a widow's dress – mention when describing a summer evening – I snatch at every word and sentence I utter, and every word you utter, too, and hurriedly lock them up in my literary pantry – in case they might come in useful!

When I finish a piece of work, I dash off to the theatre, or go off on a fishing trip, and that's the time when I ought to relax and forget myself – but no! Something that feels like a heavy cast-iron ball begins to revolve in my brain – a new subject for a novel! So immediately I drag myself back to my desk again, and I have to push on with my writing once more, to keep on writing and writing – And it's like that always, always – and I can't get any rest away from myself. I feel as though I'm devouring my own life, that for the sake of the honey I give to all and sundry I'm despoiling my best flowers of their pollen, that I'm plucking the flowers themselves and trampling on their roots. Am I out of my mind? Do you think my relatives and friends treat me like a sane person? 'What are you jotting down now? What surprises have you in store for us?' It's the same thing over and over again, until I begin to imagine that this attentiveness on the part of my friends, all this praise and admiration, is just a sham, that they are trying to deceive me just as if I were insane. Sometimes I feel afraid of them stealing up on me from behind, seizing me and carrying me off, like Poprischchin, to a lunatic asylum. As for the years when I was starting – my younger, better years – in those days my writing used to be one continuous torment. A minor writer, especially if he hasn't had much luck, sees himself as clumsy, awkward, and unwanted. He gets nervous and overwrought, and feels irresistibly drawn towards people connected with literature, or art, but then he just wanders among them unrecognized and unnoticed, unable to look them straight and courageously in the eye, like a passionate gambler who hasn't any money. I could not see my readers, but for some reason I always imagined them as unfriendly and sceptical. I was afraid of the public, it terrified me, and whenever a new play of mine was produced, I always felt that the dark-haired people in the audience were hostile to it, and the fair-haired ones coldly indifferent. Oh, how dreadful it all was! What a torment!

NINA: But even so, don't you have moments of happiness and exaltation – moments when you feel inspired, when your creative work is actually in progress?

TRIGORIN: Yes, while I'm writing I enjoy it. I enjoy reading proofs, too, but – as soon as the thing comes out in print I can no longer bear it. I immediately see that it's not what I intended, that it's a mistake, that it oughtn't to have been written at all, and I feel angry and depressed. – [*Laughing.*] And then the public reads it and says: 'Yes, it's charming, so cleverly done. – Charming, but a far cry from Tolstoy.' – Or 'A very fine piece of work, but Turgenev's *Fathers and Children* is a better book.' And so it will go on till my dying day – everything will be charming and clever – and nothing more. And when I die, my friends as they pass by my grave, will say: 'Here lies Trigorin. He was a good writer, but not as good as Turgenev.'

NINA: You must forgive me, but I refuse to try to understand you. You've simply been spoiled by success.

TRIGORIN: What success? I've never liked myself. I dislike myself as a writer. But the worst of it is that I live in a sort of haze, and I often don't understand what I'm writing. I love this water here, the trees, the sky. I have a feeling for nature, it arouses a sort of passion in me, an irresistible desire to write. But you see, I'm not a mere landscape painter, I'm also a citizen of my country; I love it, I love its people. As an author, I feel I'm in duty bound to write about the people, their sufferings, their future – and about science, the rights of man, and so on, and so forth. And I write about everything in a great hurry while I'm being prodded and urged on from all sides and people keep getting cross with me, so that I dash about from one side to the other like a fox badgered by the hounds. I see science and society forging ahead, while I drop further and further behind, like a peasant who's just missed his train, and in the end I feel that all I can do is to paint landscapes, and that everything else I write is a sham – false to the very core.

It is true that Chekhov warned his readers not to equate him with the characters he created, but with Trigorin's self-examination (for clearly Nina is there only to cue him) the temptation is too strong. Creator and character are mirrored in the lake very much as one; or so it seems to the present writer, and so it seemed to Tolstoy, although some commentators have taken Trigorin to be a portrait of the writer Potapenko. Karlinsky, in his volume of Chekhov's letters, goes even further and claims that the monologue is almost a paraphrase of a passage in Maupassant's *Sur l'eau*, though he is careful to point out that Maupassant's shallower despair and misanthropy are the very opposite of Chekhov's deep despair and compassion. Certainly the carefully observed passage suggests that if Chekhov did not actually identify with Trigorin in Act II he had an understanding of him and an underlying sympathy with him.

And so, with the many sighs of star-crossed lovers; with the tears of highly charged emotions, extravagantly expressed; with the white bones of age and the waste of young promise; with questions left unanswered and with a luminous sheet of water that separates the shores and will not free the creatures of the lakeside be they man, woman or gull, but draws them back always to its banks – the play, by one of the world's two greatest playwrights, passes before us to its sombre ending.

A closer, more penetrating look at the fabric that lies beneath the shimmering surface of *The Seagull* discovers that its main stresses are based on a series of triangles, like a group of newtown houses on stilts. Masha loves Konstantin who loves Nina. Konstantin loves Nina who loves Trigorin. Trigorin loves himself; but he conforms to the triangular pattern by loving Arkadina for a time and, for a time, Nina. And then there is Medviedenko, the conscientious and much put-upon schoolmaster, who loves – and marries – Masha, who, as we have seen, loves Konstantin, while in the background broods Polena, Sorin's bailiff and Masha's mother. She loves the doctor Dorn, who is half in love with Arkadina:

POLENA: You're so anxious to prostrate yourselves before an actress. Every single one of you!

DORN: ... It's in the nature of things for people to admire artists and treat them differently from – well, let us say, tradesmen. It's a sort of idealism.

With all this stress and strain small wonder that the surface of the lake is disturbed; that the winds whip up and lash it; and that it, in turn, seems to set up a like tempest in the souls of those it draws to its shores – storms of emotion that rise only to subside into long calm stretches of resignation and of infinite boredom – the boredom that is a part of Chekhov's great quartet of plays: the boredom of Arkadina retreating to the country; the boredom of Liubov Ranyevskaia, exiled from the Paris of her worthless young lover; the boredom of foolish, loyal, good-natured, desiccated Vanya; the boredom of three sisters, dwelling in a small provincial town but dreaming of a Moscow that never was:

IRENA: Olia, darling, I do respect the Baron. I think a lot of him, he's a very good man – I'll marry him, Olia, I'll agree to marry him, if only we can go to Moscow! Let's go, please do, let's go! There's nowhere in all the world like Moscow. Let's go, Olia! Let's go!

The good Chekhovian could do worse than ponder three

passages from *The Seagull*: the manner of the play's opening; its closing; and the underlying tensions in the first act between that arch-egoist, the actress, and her introspective son with the load of unripe talent.

Konstantin has erected his shanty stage before the lake where his mother and a small knot of admirers and her hangers-on (where is the Russian family without its fringe dependants?) have gathered by the lakeside to see his play. Arkadina, as an actress, has seen better times – nowadays when she appears it is mainly in the provinces – and so is vulnerable and insecure; she skips on to the alfresco stage to declaim, clowning:

> Oh, Hamlet, speak no more!
> Thou turn'st mine eyes into my very soul;
> And there I see such black and grained spots
> As will not leave their tinct.

To this Konstantin rejoins, equally clowning:

> And let me wring thy heart, for so I shall,
> If it be made of penetrable stuff.

Shakespeare's words could have been written to crystallize and illumine the situation between mother and son, to define their attitude to one another and incidentally to set the key of mockery in which Konstantin's offering is to be received.

Konstantin adores his mother, even as he holds her in his clear, cool sights:

TREPLIOV: It makes her angry to think that it won't be she, but Zaryechnaia, who's going to make a success of it on this tiny stage! [*Glancing at his watch.*] A psychological oddity – that's my mother. Oh, there is no doubt about her being very gifted and intelligent: she's capable of weeping bitterly over a book, of reciting the whole of Nekrasov by heart, of nursing the sick with the patience of an angel. But just try and give a word of praise to Duse! Oh-ho-ho! You mustn't praise anybody but her, you mustn't write about anybody but her, you must acclaim her and go into raptures over her wonderful acting in *The Lady of the Camellias*, or *The Fumes of Life*. But we can't offer her such intoxicating praise here in the country, so she feels bored and out of humour, and we all seem like enemies, we are all to blame. And then she's superstitious – she's afraid of having three candles alight, she's afraid of the number thirteen. And she's close-fisted, too. She has seventy thousand in the bank, in Odessa – that I know for certain. But you try to borrow money from her, and she'll just burst into tears.

But even as he highlights his mother's shortcomings to her brother, the philosophical old man, Sorin, 'Calm yourself, your mother adores you,' he is reminded.

We, with good Chekhovian hindsight, recall that in Act IV, when the ruined Nina comes back to him, her plumage tattered, out of the storm, he thinks only of his mother's peace of mind, as Nina abandons herself to the storm in the night outside: 'It won't be very nice if someone meets her [Nina] in the garden and tells Mamma. It might upset Mamma.'

One imagines that *The Seagull* would have moved to a quiet winding up, had Chekhov, so early in his career as a dramatist, had more mastery over his medium, by way, as it were, of an amen. *Uncle Vanya* has the finest of them all. The troublesome summer refugees have gone, leaving Sonia, as the good Chekhovian will remember, at her abacus in the counting-house, alone with Vanya and his old nurse, knitting a stocking in the background with Sonia's grandmother, immersed in her book. Sonia leaves her accounts to comfort Vanya, kneeling at his feet:

SONIA: We shall rest! We shall hear the angels, we shall see all the heavens covered with stars like diamonds, we shall see all earthly evil, all our sufferings swept away by the grace which will fill the whole world, and our life will become peaceful, gentle, and sweet as a caress. I believe it, I believe it. – [*Wipes his eyes with her handkerchief.*] Poor, poor Uncle Vanya, you're crying. You've had no joy in your life, but wait Uncle Vanya, wait. – We shall rest. – [*Embraces him.*] We shall rest! [*The watchman taps.*] We shall rest!

What a beautiful and masterly amen to a turbulent play.

The Three Sisters has a shorter but entirely satisfying end. The regiment has marched away, leaving the three sisters to their sorrows. Chebutikin, the old soldier, picks up his paper. He is singing softly:

CHEBUTYKIN: Tarara-boom-di-ay. – I'm sitting on a tomb-di-ay. – [*Reads the paper.*] What does it matter? Nothing matters!

OLGA: If only we knew, if only we knew!

Another perfect 'So be it' is to be found in *The Cherry Orchard*. The family has gone, leaving Feers, an aged servant, behind. They have closed the shutters and locked the door behind them, supposing that the old man has been sent to a hospital. The sound of axe blows begins. Old Feers comes tottering into the room. He is ill. He crosses to the door and tries the handle:

FEERS: Locked. They've gone. – They forgot about me. Never mind. – I'll sit here for a bit. I don't suppose Leonid Andryeevich put on his fur coat, I expect he's gone in his light one. – [*Sighs, preoccupied.*] I didn't see to *it.* – These youngsters! – My life's gone on as if I'd never lived . . . [*Lies down.*] I'll lie down a bit. You haven't got any strength left, nothing's left, nothing. – [*to himself*] Oh, you – you're daft!

Even Ibsen, superb craftsman that he was, writing a play that, like *The Seagull*, virtually ends in a gunshot, pauses for a quiet close: 'But things like this don't happen!' says Judge Brack, stunned by Hedda's violent death. Curtain. But in *The Seagull* Chekhov seems to be in a hurry to get to the end. Irena Arkadina has been playing lotto with her entourage. Frighteningly, a shot is heard. It comes from Konstantin's study, the next room, where we have seen Konstantin with Nina, before she fled back into the night. The sound breaks up the placid game:

DORN: . . . It must be something in my medicine chest that's gone off. [*Goes out through door . . . returns in half a minute.*] Just as I thought. A bottle of ether has burst . . .

ARKADINA: Ough, how it frightened me! It reminded me of how. – Everything went dark for a moment.

DORN: There was an article here about two months ago . . . [*Leads Trigorin to the footlights . . . Dropping his voice, in a lower tone.*] Take Irena Nikolayevna away from here somehow. The fact is, Konstantin Gavrilovich has shot himself.

CURTAIN

The mature Chekhov would never end so abruptly.

Chekhov wrote to his brother Mikhail from St Petersburg on 15 October 1896: 'My *Seagull* opens on 17 October. Madame Kommisarjevskaya acts amazingly.' But no sooner had the well-pleased author written home thus than the blow fell. Anton hastily wrote again to his brother:

Petersburg, October 18, 1896

The play fell through, turned out to be a complete fiasco. There was painful tension in the theatre, compounded of bewilderment and disgrace. The actors played infamously, stupidly.

The moral: one should not write plays.

Nevertheless, I am alive, well, and eupeptic.

There was, too, a letter for Suvorin written on the same day:

Petersburg, October 18, 1896

Stop the printing of the play. I shall never forget yesterday evening. But still I slept well, and am setting off in a very tolerable good-humour. I am not going to produce the play in Moscow. I shall never again write plays or have them acted.

Meanwhile Suvorin was busily writing off to Chekhov, and their letters must have crossed, for Chekhov wrote:

October 22, 1896, Melikhovo

In your last letter (dated October 18th) you thrice call me an old woman and say I was a coward. Why the libel? After the play I dined at Romanov's, as was fitting, then went to sleep, slept well and the next day left for home without pronouncing a single syllable in complaint. If I had acted the coward I would have dashed from one editor to another, from one actor to another, nervously begged their condescension, nervously introduced useless changes and would have spent another two or three weeks in St Petersburg, running back and forth to performances of my 'Seagull' in a dither, drenched in cold sweat, complaining . . . Why, when you visited me the night after the show, you yourself said it would be better for me to leave . . . So where is the cowardice? I acted just as reasonably and coolly as a man who has proposed, been turned down, and has nothing left to do but leave. Yes my vanity was wounded . . . Back home I gave myself a dose of castor oil, took a cold bath – and now I wouldn't even mind doing another play . . . My sister hurried home from St Petersburg, probably feeling that I would hang myself.

Clearly the first night of *The Seagull* had been a traumatic affair for the sensitive dramatist.

Why did this play, a masterpiece, as we now see, meet with disaster? The answer is simple enough: it attracted the wrong audience at its first performance. Not that it is alone among masterpieces in being undervalued at its first performance. Stravinsky's *Rite of Spring* and Bizet's *Carmen* are two which spring instantly to mind. (Shock at the latter was held to account for Bizet's untimely death, although it was known that the composer already had a heart condition.)

The first-night audience which gathered at the Empress Alexandra Theatre in St Petersburg on 17 October booed *The Seagull* through a shock of disappointment. Yelizaveta Levkeyeva, a popular *farceuse*, appeared in it for her Benefit performance, and the audience she drew, knowing Chekhov only for the more comical of his sketches and stories, assembled to see a riot of farce. One cannot help feeling that the result, which a little managerial *savoir-faire* would have avoided, might have been foreseen.

Chekhov himself, who at the outset had doubts about his play – 'It's nothing to ooh and aah about' – was as bitter about its failure as one of his nature could be: 'I am calm now, back to normal. But I still cannot forget what happened, any more than I could have forgotten had they punched me in the face.' The people with whom he had enjoyed carefree dinners, friends and colleagues in whose defence he had tilted with many a lance, 'all wore peculiar expressions on their faces, extremely peculiar expressions'. His colleague, Leykin, noted in his journal: 'The papers are solemnly announcing the failure of Chekhov's *Seagull* with a note of gloating. You'd think they'd finally caught a wolf who had massacred a herd of cattle.' He also noted that the drama critic of the *St Petersburg Gazette* all but hopped with joy.

Even though the St Petersburg fiasco (five performances) was followed by a great success in Kiev, Chekhov continued to feel that he was not God's gift to the drama. Did not Tolstoy complain that *The Seagull* was nothing but damped-down Ibsen, with no plot and watery characters? As it happened, Chekhov did not like Ibsen as a dramatist, although he placed his gift for writing very high. He thought him dry, cold, a man of reason.

But there were those among the audience who were more discerning, as the reply to a letter from Elena Shavrova shows:

November 1, 1896, Melikhovo
Esteemed Lady, if, as 'one of the audience', you are writing about the first performance, permit me – yes, permit me – to doubt your sincerity. You hurry to pour healing balm on the author's wounds, assuming that in the circumstances this would be better and more needed than sincerity; you are kind, sweet mask, very kind, and the feeling does honour to your heart. I did not see everything at the first performance, but what I did see was vague, dingy, dreary and wooden. I had no hand in assigning the parts, I wasn't given any new scenery, there were only two rehearsals, the actors didn't know their parts – and the result was general panic, utter depression of spirit; even Kommisarjevskaya's performance was nothing much, though her playing at one of the rehearsals was so prodigious that people in the orchestra [stalls] wept and blew their noses . . . creating a play is like wading into a mineral bath, certain that it will be warm, and then being shocked by the fact that it is cold . . . I have a sensation of nothingness, past and present.

Friends, too, must have rallied to Chekhov:

November 11, 1896, Melikhovo
You cannot imagine [wrote Chekhov to A. F. Koni] how

happy your letter made me. I saw only the first two acts of my play from the front, after that I kept in the wings, feeling all the time 'The Seagull' would be a failure. The night of the performance and the day after people asserted I had created nothing but idiots ... I left St Petersburg brimming with doubts ... I felt that if I had written and staged a play so obviously crammed with monstrous defects, I had lost all my senses and my machinery had apparently broken down for good. I was back home when I heard from St Petersburg that the second and third performances were successful; I got several letters, signed and anonymous, praising the play and scolding the critics; I read them with a sense of pleasure but still I was ashamed and peeved, and the thought lodged itself in my head that if good people found it necessary to console me, my affairs must be going badly. But your letter had a galvanizing effect upon me. I have known you for a long time, esteem you profoundly and have more faith in you than in all the critics put together ... I am quite calm now and can already think back on the play and the performance itself without revulsion.

Komissarjevskaya is a marvellous actress. At one of the rehearsals many people were teary-eyed as they watched her and remarked that she was the best actress in Russia at the present time; but at the performance she too succumbed to the prevailing mood of hostility toward my 'Seagull' and was intimidated by it, as it were, and her voice failed her. Our press treats her coldly, an attitude she does not merit, and I am sorry for her ...

Nemirovich-Danchenko – a man who was to have a profound effect on Chekhov's plays later, at the Moscow Art Theatre, wrote, too, to try to sustain the winged dramatist, sending better news of the subsequent performances. Chekhov replied:

Melikhovo
November 20th 1896

Yes, my *Seagull* was a decided failure in Petersburg at the first performance. The theatre was full of anger, the air tense with contempt. And I, following the laws of physics, shot out of Petersburg like a bomb. You and Shombatov are to blame for this since you incited me to write the play.

The picture of that disastrous first night, in spite of the way friends fought to disguise it, falls into place like a piece from a jigsaw in Chekhov's letter to V. V. Bilibin:

Melikhovo
November 1896

Of course I am glad, very glad, but after all, the success of a second and a third performance cannot erase from my soul the impressions of the first. I did not stay through it all, but what I saw was sad and strange to a degree . . . they had all lost spirit – even Kommissarjevskaya. And it was as hot as hell in the theatre. Everything was against the play. But none the less I can serve as an example to green youth – after the performance I supped at Romanov's, slept soundly all night, did not read the critique the next day (the newspaper bore an ominous look), and at mid-day made off to Moscow.

Chekhov's diary now takes up the story:

December 4, 1896

It is true I ran from the theatre, but only when the play was already over. During two or three acts I sat in L's dressing-room. There came to her in the entr'actes various theatrical officials in uniform, and wearing their orders – P. with a star! One young and handsome official came in from the government police. When a person is attracted to an art which is foreign to his temperament he invariably turns into an official. So many people, through the impossibility of ever becoming an artist, clutch at the fringe of the profession, a parasite in uniform. It is all that they can do.

Chekhov was grateful to his rallying friends, even though he blinked away the well-meaning mist with which they sought to shield his inner eye from a wilderness of disaster. The following extract is from a letter to A. S. Suvorin:

Melikhovo, December 14, 1896

You and Koni have brought me not a few fine moments with your letters, but just the same my soul feels exactly as if it were zinc-lined.

The flight of the seagull, then, had come to rest for a time, but not for ever. Two years later it was mounted by the Moscow Art Theatre, where it scored the triumph its author so richly deserved.

In answer to Nemirovich-Danchenko's telegram telling him of the success of the first night, Chekhov wired his 'heartfelt gratitude': '. . . Am stuck in Yalta like Dreyfus on Devil's Island. Wish I were with you. Your telegram made me healthy and happy.' Danchenko's telegram was followed by confirmation in the form of a letter from Kommisarjevskaya

St Petersburg
October 21, 1898

I have just returned from the Theatre, dear Anton Pavlovich. Victory is ours.

The play is a complete success, just as it should be, in fact just as it had to be. How I would like to see you now [Chekhov was in Yalta, sent there under doctor's orders] but what I'd like even more is for you to be present and hear the unanimous cry of 'Author'. Your – no – our *Seagull*, because I have merged with her for ever heart and soul – is alive; her sufferings and fate are so ardent that she will compel many others to have faith; 'Think of your vocation and have no fear of life'.

I clasp your hand,

V. Kommisarjevskaya

On 19 January Chekhov was able to report to the actress from Yalta, albeit sadly: 'Eight performances of my *Seagull* have already been given in Moscow. I am told the performance is extraordinary and that the cast has an excellent grasp of the roles . . . Be that as it may, I no longer want to write plays. The theatre in Petersburg cured me of that.' His disillusion with the theatre is revealed in a letter he wrote to Suvorin:

November 25, 1899

Our actors never observe ordinary people. They know nothing of landowners, business men, priests, or civil servants. On the other hand, they are quite capable of playing billiard-markers, rich men's mistresses, drunken card-sharpers, and all those characters they chance to observe incidentally during their drinking bouts. The real trouble with actors is their abysmal ignorance.

Stanislavski, in his book *My Life in Art*, has left us a description of the Moscow Art Theatre's struggle within itself to launch *The Seagull* on its second flight in the company's first season. It was the second notable production of *The Seagull*. In the two-year gap that followed the St Petersburg fiasco, the play had been mounted in several provincial theatres.

. . . After my first acquaintance with Chekhov's *Seagull* I did not understand the essence, the aroma, the beauty of his play. I wrote the *mise-en-scène* and still I did not understand, although, unknown to myself, I had apparently felt its substance. When I directed the play I still did not understand it. But some of the inner threads of the play attracted me, although I did not notice the evolution that had taken place in me . . .

Apparently there are many ways to the hidden riches, to the entrance into the soul of the play, the roles, and the actors who play them.

Chekhov showed some reluctance to allow Stanislavski and his director, Nemirovich-Danchenko, to mount the play in so important an artistic centre as Moscow, for on 12 May Danchenko was writing to him: 'Why will you not authorize our production? After all, *The Seagull* is playing all over the country. Why can we not do it in Moscow? The enthusiastic reviews in the Karkhov and Odessa newspapers are quite unprecedented.'

And then, ten days later, suddenly, or so it seemed, Chekhov saw the light and allowed Stanislavski and Nemirovich-Danchenko to present any of his plays they liked.

The conditions under which we produced *The Seagull* were complex and hard. The production was necessary to us because of the material circumstances of the life of our theatre. Business was in a bad way. The administration hurried our labours. And suddenly Anton Pavlovich [Chekhov] fell ill in Yalta with a new attack of tuberculosis. His spiritual condition was such that if *The Seagull* should fail as it did at its first production in Petrograd [St Petersburg], the great poet would not be able to weather the blow. His sister Maria Pavlovna [Masha to us] warned us of this with tears in her eyes, when, on the eve of the performance, she begged us to postpone it. You can judge of the condition in which we actors played on the first night before a small but chosen audience. There were only six hundred roubles in the box office. When we were on the stage there was an inner whisper in our hearts: 'You must play well, you must play better than well; you must create not only success, but triumph, for know that if you do not, the man and writer you love will die, killed by your hands.'

These inner whisperings did not aid our creative inspiration. [One can well believe this.] The boards were becoming the floor of a gallows, and we actors the executioners.

. . . The first act was over. There was a gravel-like silence. Knipper [later Chekhov's wife] fainted on the stage. All of us could hardly keep our feet. In the throes of despair we began moving to our dressing-rooms. Suddenly there was a roar in the auditorium, and a shriek of joy or fright on the stage. The curtain was lifted, fell, was lifted again . . . and we could not even gather sense enough to bow.

In the spring of 1899, his illness conquered for a time, Chekhov arrived in Moscow and demanded that the Art Theatre should give it again for him to see: 'Listen, it is necessary for me. I am its author. How can I write anything else [for the theatre] until I have seen it?'

The special performance was given in the Nikitsky Theatre, the Moscow Art Theatre being in the throes of the summer closing and the annual cleaning and refurbishing. It was attended by Chekhov and about ten other people in the audience. 'The impression [we gave the author] was only middling,' wrote Stanislavski. 'After every act Chekhov ran on the stage and his face bore no signs of any inner joy'. Chekhov's candid account of his feelings about the production at the special performance were set out in a letter to Maxim Gorki:

Melikhovo,
May 9, 1899

I used to enjoy hunting small game, but it doesn't attract me any more. I saw *Seagull* without any sets. I can't judge the play with equanimity, because the seagull herself [Roxcemovo] gave such an abominable performance – she blubbered loudly throughout – and the Trigorin [Stanislavski] walked around the stage and spoke like a paralytic. He is not supposed to have 'a will of his own', but the way the actor conveyed it was nauseating to behold. It wasn't bad on the whole, though, quite gripping in fact. There were moments when I found it hard to believe I had written it . . .

The fact that *The Seagull* had been the theatrical event of the year did not soften Chekhov's approach to it. He found fault with the production's sound effects and felt the movement of *ensemble* to be distracting. He was to lose all patience with the weepy Nina and demanded to have her replaced.

Stanislavski gives an interesting view, not always adhered to, of the author Trigorin. Chekhov, it seemed to him, tried to avoid him on his dashes to the stage at this special performance.

. . . I waited for him in my dressing-room, but he did not come. This was a bad sign. I went to him myself.

'Scold me, Anton Pavlovich,' I begged him.

'Wonderful! Listen, it was wonderful! Only you need torn shoes and checked trousers.'

. . . I played the part in the most elegant of costumes [and so did Gielgud in the 1936 production of M. Kommisarjevsky] . . .

A year or more passed . . . and during one of the performances I [in white trousers, white vest, white hat, slippers, and a handsome make-up] suddenly understood what Chekhov had meant.

Of course, the shoes must be torn and the trousers checked . . .

(But from this point onwards a nagging doubt haunts the present writer which will not be silenced: would the eminently presentable Arkadina, whose dresses cost a fortune, it will be remembered, have allowed Trigorin to be reduced, in her entourage, to torn shoes? Would she not smother him in new shoes, new suits, as a part of an unspoken arrangement?) Certainly in the current production of the Russian film, Trigorin looks as though his suit had been bought off the peg some seasons ago.

December 30, 1902

Dear Sergei Pavlovich [Diaghilev],

I have received *The World of Art* with the *Seagull* article and read the article. Thank you very much. When I finished the article, I felt like writing a play, and I probably will after January ...

Present-day culture is the beginning of work in the name of a great future, work which will perhaps continue for tens of thousands of years with the result that finally, if only in the distant future, mankind will perceive the truth of the real God, that is, not make conjectures or search for Him as in Dostoyevsky, but perceive Him as clearly as they perceive that two times two is four ...

Happy New Year, and all the best.

Your devoted,

A. Chekhov

Chekhov's characters live in that darkness that comes before the dawn, but his vision is no vision of despair. Nothing that happens or does not happen can shake his trust in the dawning of the day. ' ... all the plays of Chekhov are permeated [with] and end in a faith in a better future ... ,' observed Stanislavski. It is an observation from which, however, *The Seagull*, by its very nature, its symbolism and its widest intention, must be excluded.

Where is the hope that Konstantin will some day find himself in his writing, when, because he recognizes his failure to do so, he kills himself? And there is no hope now that the morally bedraggled Nina, rushing blindly back into that night of storm and fate, will ever be the actress that she might have been – she will dip in her flight lower and lower, to be submerged and sink without trace. There is no hope that Arkadina will hold the man she loves. In fact the only one of the principal quartet in the play who is certain to survive, and indeed thrive, is that instrument of fate, the morally and artistically indefensible Trigorin, who has been the ruin of them all. It is in this sad certainty that the curtains of their fate fall, leaving only the truth of the tragedy to console the onlooker. Chekhov, like no other writer, creates and combines his own inner truth with outer appearances, which is why each time, each production is less a play than an experience, and the good Chekhovian, be he player or director or playgoer, keeps the beacons burning in the four great lighthouses, *The Seagull, Uncle Vanya, The Cherry Orchard,* and *The Three Sisters.*

Uncle Vanya

Before embarking upon Chekhov's early, blemished play, *The Wood Demon*, and upon *Uncle Vanya*, in which he beautifully crystallized the earlier piece's sprawling, dawdling contours, we could do worse than remind ourselves that inside every Russian of the landed classes of his day was a degree in forestry trying to get out.

Both plays deal with the same main characters, though the cast list of thirteen in *The Wood Demon* is magically reduced to a cast of seven in *Uncle Vanya*. The play glows the more for the compression.

James Agate defined *Uncle Vanya* as 'an embroidery upon the theme of apprenticeship to sorrow', quoting, in his habitually immaculate French, his source: 'L'homme est un apprenti, la douleur est son Maître.'

The date of 6 October 1897 finds Chekhov writing to Lydia Avilova from Nice:

You deplore the fact that my characters are gloomy. Alas, it isn't my fault! This happens involuntarily, and when I write I don't think I am lugubrious; at any rate, I am always in a good mood while I work. It has been pointed out that sombre, melancholy people always write gaily, while the works of cheerful souls are always depressing. But I am a joyous person; at least I have lived the first thirty years of my life at my ease, as they say.

My health is tolerable in the morning and excellent at night. I am not doing anything, don't write and don't feel like writing. I have become frightfully lazy.

The weather is magnificent here [he was writing to Suvorin from Nice on 13 March 1898], sheer enchantment. Warm, even hot; the sky blue, bright, the sea sparkling, the fruit trees in blossom . . . I have grown lazy as an Arab, and I do nothing, absolutely nothing . . . I am more than ever firmly convinced that a Russian can't work and be his ownself unless the weather is wretched.

You have grown attached to the theatre, but apparently I retire from it further and further – and I am sorry, for in the past the theatre gave me much that was good (and it gives me a fairly good income; this winter my plays were successful as never before in the provinces, even *Uncle Vanya*). Formerly I had no greater delight than to sit in a theatre, but now I sit there feeling as though at any moment someone in the gallery will shout: 'Fire!' And I don't like actors. This change is due to my being a playwright . . .

On 3 December 1898 he wrote to Alexei Makinovich [Maxim Gorki] from Yalta: 'I wrote *Uncle Vanya* a very long time ago. I have never seen it staged. In the last few years it has often been produced in provincial theatres, perhaps because I included it in my volume of collected plays. I feel indifferent toward all my plays and have long since ceased following the theatre. I have no desire to write for the theatre any more.'

It has been said that while Chekhov could see a poetic and subtle Gorki who did not in truth exist, Gorki kept telling Chekhov his writing was brutal. Yet he loved and admired *Uncle Vanya* and *The Cherry Orchard: 'Uncle Vanya* is a completely new species of dramatic art, it is a hammer with which you pound on the public's empty heads.' He then went on to liken this, to our eyes, gentle play to a pig that he once saw destroying a flowerbed. Gorki also saw in Chekhov what he took to be an indifference to human suffering – in Chekhov, the most affectionate and compassionate of men and writers. 'You know,' he wrote, 'I feel that in this play you are colder than the devil to human beings. You are as indifferent to them as snow, as a blizzard.'

Earlier Chekhov had written to his brother Michel from Yalta, on 26 October 1898. Half-ruefully, he noted: 'My *Uncle Vanya* is being performed throughout the provinces and is a success everywhere. So you see, one never knows where he'll make it and where he won't.'

On 22 February 1899 he wrote to I. I. Orlov from Yalta: 'No news of any particular note.' Chekhov, who found the work of revising particularly unattractive and, as we know, had already conceived *Uncle Vanya* in the somewhat unwieldy form of *The Wood Demon*, evidently thought the news of *Vanya*'s forthcoming production in Moscow small *qvass*. 'Next season a play of mine [*Vanya*] that has never appeared in the capitals before will be performed at the Maly Theater . . .'

The Maly Theater. As things turned out it was less a slip between the Maly cup and the Chekhovian lip than an almighty artistic gap.

Although Chekhov had been pleased with the success at the Moscow mounting of *The Seagull* there were aspects of the Nemirovich-Danchenko production, and in particular of some of the casting, that had disturbed him. And so, when the Moscow Art Theatre applied for *Uncle Vanya,* Chekhov's response was to send it to the theatre of the Establishment. At the government-run and tradition-bound Maly, *Uncle Vanya,* like every other play submitted, was required to pass the scrutiny of a government-appointed literary committee. There, as might have been foreseen, Chekhov's delicate tracery of summer's sun and shadow and the laughter that glinted Aprilwise through the tears was, to put it bluntly, turned down. The government committee found the play 'dramatically unsound and socially irrelevant', wherefore it was pronounced unfit for performance at an Imperial Theatre unless Chekhov were to revise it according to their specifications.

The dramatist, like many another after – and no doubt before – him, promptly executed a *volte-face* and sent the play to the Moscow Art Theatre.

'Little action, a ton of love,' we remember, Chekhov jotted down in his notebook. He happened to be writing *The Seagull* at the time, but the same observation might well apply to any or all of his high quartet of plays, and perhaps particularly to *Uncle Vanya.* 'In Chekhov's plays as in life,' George Meredith reminds us, 'passions spin the plot.' Its very subtitle, *Scenes from Country Life,* a title which came from a reading of Ostrovsky, suggests plenty of leisure for love-making.

The scene is set in a family house deep in the country. Here four drifting lovers agonize and part while we, who watch the lengthening shadow of their pyramid of predicaments, laugh and are sad with them, which is of course what their creator intended.

'Did you ever have that feeling that you wanted to go, and yet that you wanted to stay?' So, however unknowingly, Schnozzle

Durante put the central problem of the Family Serebriakov to us in a song. I do not believe that anyone has ever stated it more lucidly.

The pyramid might be said to begin with Serebriakov, an ailing and aged professor (. . . 'to have to meet stupid people every day, to have to listen to their trivial conversation . . . It's more than I can bear! And they won't even forgive me for getting old!'), and his elegant and languorous young wife, Yeliena – *la Seconde*. ('How lovely *she* is! How lovely!' 'Is she faithful to the Professor?' 'I am sorry to say she is.'). They have retired to the country home of the professor's first wife ('a beautiful, gentle creature, as pure as that blue sky, generous and noble-hearted'), obliged to abandon their pleasant but spendthrift metropolitan existence because their money has run out. On the estate lives the family household, which consists of Marina, Uncle Vanya's ancient childhood nurse:

> (MARINA: [*nods her head disapprovingly*] Such goings-on! The professor gets up at midday, but the samovar is kept boiling the whole morning waiting for him. Before they came we always had dinner soon after twelve, like everybody else, but now they are here we have it after six in the evening. The professor spends the night reading and writing and then suddenly, past one o'clock, the bell rings – My goodness, what is it? He wants some tea! So you've got to wake people up to heat the samovar – Such goings-on!
> ASTROV: Are they going to stay here much longer?
> VANYA: [*whistles*] A hundred years maybe! The professor's decided to settle here.)

and Maryia Vassilievna Voinitskaia, the elderly intellectual, the mother of the professor's first wife ('For some reason you don't like listening when I talk') and the worn-out demon that is Astrov, a man in love with trees:

(ASTROV: . . . Nanny, how many years is it we've known each other?

MARINA: [*pondering*] . . . The Lord help my memory . . . Sonechka's mother . . . was still living then . . . That means at least eleven years have gone by . . .

ASTROV: Have I changed a lot since then?

MARINA: Yes, a lot. You were young and handsome then, but . . . you're not as good looking as you were . . .

ASTROV: Yes – In ten years I've become a different man.)

and Sonia, the professor's good, self-sacrificing, honest but plain daughter: ('I dare say I'm just as unhappy as you are [Uncle Vanya] but I don't despair all the same. I bear it, and I shall continue to bear it till my life comes to its natural end').

Maurice Valency argues that Chekhov did not choose Yeliena's name at random. He postulates that the writer had in mind that other Helen who set the world by the ears, and who, after each travail, returned in the end to a husband she despised. The difference is that Chekhov's Helen has no Paris, no Troy, no adventure and no epic.

Then there is Uncle Vanya, Voinitsky, Sonia's Uncle Vanya, and the professor's brother-in-law by his first marriage: ('Day and night I feel suffocated by the thought that my life has been irretrievably lost. I have no past – it has all been stupidly wasted on trifles – while the present is awful because it's so meaningless.') Man proposes; God disposes, as the old saying is, and during the play we shall see the proverb working out.

In addition to these characters is Telyeghin, a neighbour, called 'Waffles' because of the pock-marks on his face:

TELYEGHIN: Forgive me, Vanya. My wife ran away from me the day after our wedding with a man she loved – because of my unprepossessing appearance. But even after that I never failed in my duty towards her. I still love her; I'm faithful to her . . . I've spent all I possessed on educating the children she had by the man she loved. I've lost my happiness, but I've still got my pride. And what about her? Her youth is gone, her beauty has faded, as nature ordains that it must, the man she loved has died – What has she got left?'

Uncle Vanya is the first play in which Chekhov held the sunshine in balance with the cloud. As in *Platonov*, Chekhov has looked about him and caught a neighbour, here; a young girl married to an old man, there; a mother-in-law, advanced in age, admiring her pseudo-intellectual elderly son-in-law, the professor, and disapproving of the younger generation in general and of her own son, Vanya, in particular; a favourite, if unpractical uncle, a dashing young demon on the way to becoming a burned-out old pantaloon – a rocket on the downward path of its arc – and a pious and rather plain young woman, lost in her dream of the demon doctor. Chekhov has used his eyes, his ears, his affectionate laughter and his inalienable compassion; he has in fact sent in the clowns and, clown-like, they have shown us their vulnerable hearts even as we smile at their antics. Yet Chekhov's vision, stripped of sentimentality, of these figures in a hot summer in rural Russia is dedicated to truth.

With this play we find that Chekhov has quietly donned the mantle of the social historian, specializing in middle-class lassitude. Writing short stories of no more than one thousand words, sardonic or sad and usually both, for the editor N. A. Leikin, from the outset of his career conditioned him well to look at pathos through the eyes of gentle laughter and to mock even those he found endearing, a genial uncle to humanity. He turned every play he was to write, from *Uncle Vanya* onwards, into tragi-comedy.

The play opens in a garden one sultry afternoon. Its very heaviness suggests the storm that will break that night, both in the air the household breathes and in their emotions. It is a heavy and a laden air which seeps into the silences, and they are many, in the scene.

> VOINITSKY [Vanya]: It's hot and close, but our great man of learning has got his overcoat and goloshes on, and he's carrying his umbrella and gloves.

From this single speech and the manner of its delivery we are made aware, if our eyes have not already told us so, that the professor is a *malade*, probably *imaginaire* – soon we are to learn that we have been right:

> ASTROV: [*to Yeliena*] You know I've come to see your husband. You wrote and told me that he was very ill – rheumatism and something else – but I find that he's perfectly well.
> YELIENA: Last night he was depressed and complained of pains in his legs, but today he seems all right . . .
> ASTROV: And I've galloped twenty miles at breakneck speed . . .

There is little love lost between Vanya and his brother-in-law.

We have yet to know that the professor is married to an exquisite young wife, Yeliena. And almost immediately we are to learn that Vanya is in one of his dustiest moods:

> VOINITSKY: Everything's old, I'm just the same as I was – perhaps worse, because I've grown lazy: I don't do anything, I just grumble like some old fogey. As for my *Maman*, the old magpie still goes on chattering about the emancipation of women. With one eye she looks into her grave and with the other she studies her learned books looking for the dawn of a new life.

And so already we know not only that Vanya is introspective, in sharp contradiction to the grumble-gutting of his old nurse, who is concerned only with the surfaces of living, but that his elderly *Maman* is indomitable.

If we turn back to the scene between Astrov and Marina we shall know a great deal, though by no means all there is to know, about the demon of decay that possesses him – the dichotomy of the doctor being the twofold demon: a) of decay and b) of the inverse side of the Astrov coin, the smouldering desire to create by planting trees. But at the opening of the play we are concerned only with the decay of the man of medicine:

ASTROV: In ten years I've become a different man. And what's the cause of it? I've been working too hard, Nanny. I'm on my feet from morning till night – I never have any peace. At night as I lie under the blankets I feel afraid all the time that I may be dragged out to see a patient. During the whole time you and I have known each other I haven't had a single day. How could I help ageing? Besides, the life itself is tedious, stupid, squalid – this sort of life drags you down . . . Ugh!, what a huge moustache I've grown – Silly moustache! I've become an eccentric, Nanny . . . My brains are still functioning all right, but my feelings are somewhat duller. I don't wish for anything [nothing he wished for, forsooth! only the professor's languorous wife, we are to find in due course], I don't feel I need anything, I don't love anybody. Except you perhaps – I believe I'm fond of you. I had a Nanny like you when I was a child . . . in the first week of Lent I went to Malitskoe, because of the epidemic – spotted typhus – In the huts you could hardly move for sick people – Dirt, stench, and smoke everywhere – and calves mixed up with the sick on the floor – Young pigs there as well. I struggled with it all day, hadn't a moment to sit down or to swallow a bite of food. But would they let me rest when I got home? No, they brought me a signalman from the railway. I laid him on the table to operate, and he went and died on me under the chloroform. And just when I least wanted it my feelings seemed to wake up again, and my conscience began to worry me as if I had killed him deliberately – I sat down, closed my eyes – just like this – and I started to think. [And here, thus early, comes the message of Chekhov's high quartet] I wondered whether the people who come after us in a hundred years' time, the people for whom we are now blasting a trail – would they remember us and speak kindly of us? No, Nanny, I'd wager they won't!

MARINA: If people won't remember, God will.

And so, in a handful of opening speeches and with a compression that Ibsen could well have envied, we have been made aware of the probable course of the stresses in Vanya. A young wife, ripe for the plucking – we have yet to meet her – married to an old man, with two admirers, in the sultry heat of the country. But we have still to be aware of Sonia and her part in the interplay of characters.

Soon Sonia gives herself away to everyone save the doctor.

Sonia, a plain, gauche, impulsive, pious girl, loves Astrov, the doctor and man of trees.

SONIA: [alone] He didn't say anything to me – His soul and his heart are still hidden from me, so why do I feel so happy? [Laughs with happiness.] I told him: you have poise and nobility of mind and such a soft voice – Did it sound out of place? His voice vibrates and caresses – I can almost feel it in the air now. But when I said that to him about a younger sister, he didn't understand.

Did Chekhov's Sonia echo the avowal device from Shakespeare's Viola?

> My father had a daughter loved a man,
> As it might be, perhaps, were I a woman
> I should your lordship.

But back to Sonia:

> [*Wringing her hands.*] Oh, how dreadful it is that I'm not good-looking! How dreadful! I know I'm plain, I know, I know! – Last Sunday as people were coming out of church I heard them talking about me and a woman said: 'She's kind and generous, but what a pity she is so plain.'

When the play opens Sonia is at odds with her young step-mother, though we, in the audience, may not yet be aware of this. Wrongly she suspects Yeliena of having married her father for his, on the whole, ill-founded position in provincial society.

> YELIENA: You're cross with me because you think I married your father for ulterior motives – If you are impressed by oaths, I'll vow to you that I married him for love. I was attracted by him as a learned man, a celebrity. It wasn't real love, it was all artificial, but you see at that time it seemed real to me. I'm not to blame.

And again, in an earlier scene:

> VOINITSKY: If only you could see your face, your movements! – You give the impression that life is too much of an effort for you – Oh, such an effort!
> YELIENA: Oh, yes, such an effort and such a bore! Everyone blames my husband, everyone looks at me with compassion: an unfortunate woman – she's got an old husband!

It is fascinating to see Yeliena, *femme – malgré elle fatale*, through her own eyes and then to look at her through the eyes of another. First Yeliena as she sees herself:

> YELIENA: . . . I'm just a tiresome person of no importance. In my music studies, in my home life in my husband's house, in all my romantic affairs – in everything I've just been a person of no importance. Really, Sonia, when you come to think of it, I'm a very very unfortunate woman . . .

And now through the eyes of Astrov, of whom she has said:

> YELIENA: The doctor has a tired, sensitive face. An interesting face. Sonia is obviously attracted by him . . . I understand her feelings. He's visited the house three times since I've been here, but I'm shy and haven't once had a proper talk with him . . .

Astrov, the man of trees with the 'tired, sensitive face', sees himself differently from the genius Yeliena comes to recognize in him:

> ASTROV: You know, when you walk through a forest on a dark night and you see a small light gleaming in the distance, you don't notice your tiredness, nor the darkness, nor the sharp prickly branches lashing you in the face – I work harder than anyone in the district – you know that – fate batters me continuously, at times I suffer unbearably – but there's no small light in the distance . . .

And now we see Yeliena through the eyes of the man with 'no small light in the distance', as he speaks of what is beginning to seem to him a wasted summer.

> ASTROV: You just happened to come along with your husband and all of us here, who'd been working and running around and trying to create something, we all had to drop

everything and occupy ourselves wholly with you and your husband's gout. You two infected all of us with your indolence. I was attracted by you and I've done nothing for a whole month, and in the meantime people have been ill and the peasants have been using my woods, my plantations of young trees as pasture for their cattle ... wherever you and your husband go, you bring along destruction with you ... I'm convinced that if you'd stayed on here the devastation would have been immense ...

This is no picture of a secondary character. Nor does the languorous woman seen through the eyes of Vanya subscribe to her description of herself:

VANYA: [to *Yeliena*] ... You are my happiness, my life, my youth ... only let me look at you and hear your voice ... Let me talk of my love ... that in itself will be such great happiness to me.

All in all Yeliena emerges to us as Woman – not a woman, but all lovely, troubled women. To each she mirrors the Yeliena she thinks they see. Perhaps by her indolent nature she is too languorous to make the effort to be herself. She seems, in fact, to have no self. Yet in the truth at the heart of Chekhov's creation she is authentic – a *jeune fille bien élevée* trapped in her marriage to an old and petulant husband:

SEREBRIAKOV: I dozed off just now and I dreamt that my left leg didn't belong to me ...

They say Turgenev got *angina pectoris* from gout. I'm afraid I might get it. This damnable, disgusting old age! The devil take it! Since I've aged so much I've become revolting even to myself. And you find it revolting to look at me – all of you!

Yeliena, who has been up with him, much in this frame of mind, for two nights running, and with what must seem to her to be an infinity of such nights ahead lying in wait to trap her, catches his querulous tone. She is his chattel. She sighs:

YELIENA: You talk of your old age in a tone of voice which suggests we're all to blame for it.

SEREBRIAKOV: You are the first to find me repulsive ... You're young, healthy, good-looking, you want to live – whereas I am an old man, almost a corpse ... Of course, it's stupid of me to go on living. But wait a little while ... I shan't have to linger on much longer.

YELIENA: [*resigned*] Wait a little, have patience! In five or six years I shall be old, too.

To summarize: in Act I we meet the family Voinitsky and their entourage on a sultry summer's afternoon. The storm, which the oppressive atmosphere has presaged, breaks in Act II, in which we find that the professor, as usual, has the entire household up in the middle of the night. We realize that he is afraid of Vanya, on whom he depends for the upkeep of his first wife's estate, which provides the income on which he lives. The wildly funny end of Act III proves, in its own way, that the professor's fear of Vanya is not totally unfounded, for Vanya tries to shoot him and misses – twice.

VOINITSKY: Missed? Missed again! [*Furiously.*] Damnation! devil – devil take it! [*Flings the revolver on the floor and sinks on to a chair, exhausted* ...] Oh, what have I done? What am I doing?

One feels instinctively that had the telephone been in general use, Vanya would infallibly have got the wrong number.

But before this the storm of Act II breaks, buffeting the all-too-vulnerable emotions of the household – your Russki of the *ancien régime* buffeted somewhat easily:

VOINITSKY: There's a storm getting up. [*A flash of lightning.*] There, did you see? Hélène and Sonia, do go to bed, I've come to take your place.

SEREBRIAKOV: [*alarmed*] No, no! Don't leave me with him! Don't! He'll kill me with his talking!

VOINITSKY: But they must have some rest! It's the second night they've had no sleep.

SEREBRIAKOV: Let them go to bed, but you go too . . . I do implore you. For the sake of our past friendship, don't argue. We'll talk later on.

VOINITSKY: [*with a sneer*] Our past friendship – past . . .

SEREBRIAKOV: [*to Yeliena*] My dear, don't leave me alone with him. He'll kill me with his talking . . . Everyone's awake, everyone's worn out – [*with irony*] only I am thoroughly enjoying myself.

By now we know that two neurasthenias cobble the darning of the background of the Voinitsky household. These are: a) Vanya's depressive inertia (he might well, like the student in *The Cherry Orchard*, be nicknamed 'Two and Twenty Misfortunes'); and b) Astrov's quicksilver, driving passion for his trees and his ineradicable feeling of guilt for a patient who died under anaesthetic during a casualty operation one evening when the doctor was in an advanced state of fatigue. The storm moreover touches Vanya, an inert martyr to unrequited love, to the quick:

VOINITSKY: She's gone. [*A pause.*] Ten years ago I used to meet her [Yeliena] at my sister's house. She was seventeen then and I was thirty-seven. Why didn't I fall in love with her then and ask her to marry me? It could have been done so easily! She would have been my wife now – Yes – and we two might have been awakened by this storm; she would

have been frightened by the thunder and I would have held
her in my arms and whispered: 'Don't be afraid, I'm here.'
Oh, what a wonderful thought! How enchanting! it actually makes me laugh with happiness but, Oh, God! my
thoughts are in a tangle – Why am I so old? Why won't she
understand me? . . . And how I've been cheated! I adored
the professor, the gouty old invalid, and I worked like an ox
for him! Sonia and I squeezed all we could out of this
estate – Like close-fisted peasants we traded in linseed oil,
dried peas, and curds, we saved on our food so that we
could scrape together halfpence and farthings and send
him thousands of roubles . . . Everything he wrote or
uttered seemed to me the work of a genius . . . And I've been
cheated – I see it now – stupidly cheated.

The storm that has played havoc with the household's nervous systems subsides into a heightened calm which becomes the
background to a reconciliation – Yeliena and her stepdaughter
arrive at an emotional acceptance. They laugh a little, cry a
little and share a loving-cup with one another. Sonia confesses
her strong but secret love for Astrov, whereupon Yeliena,
woman-like, cannot leave well alone but must needs meddle and
sound out the state of the doctor's affections. Vanya leaves
Yeliena with Astrov to bring her 'Autumn roses, exquisite,
mournful roses'. Yeliena seizes her opportunity:

YELIENA: . . . I want to put you through a little interrogation,
and I feel rather embarrassed; I don't know how to begin
. . . It concerns a certain young person. We'll talk frankly,
like friends, without beating about the bush . . . Agreed?
ASTROV: Agreed.
YELIENA: The matter concerns my stepdaughter, Sonia. Tell
me, do you like her?
ASTROV: Yes, I respect her.

YELIENA: Do you like her as a woman?

ASTROV: [*after a brief pause*] No.

YELIENA: ... Have you noticed anything?

ASTROV: Nothing.

YELIENA: [*taking him by the hand*] You don't love her, I see it from your eyes – She is suffering – Understand that, and – stop coming here.

ASTROV: My time's past – Besides, I've got too much to do – When could I find time?

YELIENA: Ough! What an unpleasant conversation! I feel as though I've been carrying a ton weight about. .... Let's forget it, as if we hadn't talked at all, and – and go away. You're an intelligent man, you will understand – [*A pause*] I feel I'm quite flushed.

ASTROV: If you'd told me a month or two ago, I might perhaps have considered it, but now ... There's only one thing I don't understand: why did you have to have this interrogation? Suppose Sonia is suffering – I'm prepared to think it probable – but what was the purpose of this cross-examination? [*Preventing her from speaking, with animation.*] Please don't try to look astonished. You know perfectly well why I come here each day – Why, and on whose account ... You charming bird of prey, don't look at me like that, I'm a wise old sparrow.

YELIENA: Bird of prey! I don't understand at all!

ASTROV: A beautiful, fluffy weasel – You must have a victim! Here I've been doing nothing for a whole month. I've dropped everything, I seek you out hungrily – and you are awfully pleased about it, awfully – Well, what am I to say? I'm conquered, but you knew that without an interrogation!

YELIENA: Have you gone out of your mind?

ASTROV: How wonderful, how glorious you are! One kiss – If

I could only kiss your fragrant hair . . . Oh, how beautiful
you are! What lovely hands!

YELIENA: . . . Go away!

ASTROV: . . . Where shall we meet tomorrow? You see it's
inevitable. We must see each other.

[He kisses her and at that moment Vanya comes in with
his bunch of autumn roses, exquisite mournful roses, and
stands miserably in the doorway. After a long pause to take
the embracing couple in, he lays the roses gently on a
chair.]

VOINITSKY: Never mind – no – never mind.

It is the perfect way to conclude the little episode and tells us
more about Vanya, the pepper-and-salt man, than any of his
speeches.

Earlier Act III has disclosed one of Chekhov's strokes of wit. The
scene is set in the middle of a mild autumn day. The household is
drifting into a drawing-room, one after another, but when the
curtain rises only Vanya, Yeliena and Sonia have arrived.

'The *Herr* Professor,' says Vanya, from whose voice irony is
rarely absent, 'has graciously expressed a wish that we should
assemble in this drawing-room at one o'clock.' He inspects his
watch. 'It is a quarter to.' (Oh, admirable an unusual *fin de siècle*
trio of Russians who are not only not late, but actually a little
before time!) 'He wishes to make some communication to the
world,' he concludes drily.

'Probably some business matter,' says Yeliena incuriously.
She is, as she admits presently, 'dying of boredom'.

VOINITSKY: He does no business of any kind. He just writes
nonsense, grumbles and feels jealous – he does nothing else.

YELIENA: [*to Vanya*] And you keep droning away all the

time, all day long! Aren't you tired of it? I'm dying of
boredom – I don't know what to do.

Sonia indicates that there is plenty to do if only Yeliena cared to
do it:

SONIA: You could help in running the estate, teach children,
help to look after the sick . . . before you and papa came to
live here, Uncle Vanya and I used to go to the market
ourselves and sell the flour.

But the indolent Yeliena does not know how to do such things.

YELIENA: . . . I'm not interested. It's only in idealistic novels
that people teach and doctor the peasants . . .
SONIA: Well, I just don't understand how you can help
wanting to go and teach them. Wait a little, you'll get
accustomed to the idea . . . You're bored and you don't
know what to do with yourself, but boredom and idleness
are infectious. Look: Uncle Vanya isn't doing anything
either, just following you about like a shadow . . . The
doctor, Mihailovich, only comes to see us very rarely, used
to once a month . . . But now he comes here every day, he's
neglecting his forestry and his practice. You must be a
witch.

'Why be miserable?' Vanya asks Yeliena. 'Come, my dear,
wonderful woman, be sensible!' [Not the strongest part of any
Russian of Chekhov's creation, one remembers. Even Lopakhin
in *The Cherry Orchard* has his lapses from good sense.] 'A mermaid's blood flows in your veins, so be a mermaid! Let yourself
go for once in your life! Fall head over heels in love with some
water-sprite – and plunge head first into deep water, so that the
Herr Professor and all of us just throw up our hands in amaze-
ment!' 'Even an angel couldn't hold her patience with you,' is

Yeliena's petulant reply.

The professor enters with Telyeghin, who seems to have got in before him with his list of ailments:

TELYEGHIN: I'm not feeling too well myself, your Excellency. I've been poorly for the last two days. Something the matter with my head ...

SEREBRIAKOV [the professor]: ... I don't like this house. It's like a sort of labyrinth. Twenty-six enormous rooms ... and there's no finding anyone ... One can put up with ill health, after all. But what I can't stomach is the whole pattern of life in the country. I feel as if I had been cast off the earth on to some strange planet ... I beg you, my friends, lend me your ears, as the saying goes. [*Laughs.*] [*No one else does*].

VOINITSKY: [*agitated*] Maybe I'm not needed here? Can I go?

SEREBRIAKOV: No, you're needed more than anyone ... Why – are you annoyed at something? If I've offended you in any way, please excuse me.

VOINITSKY: You needn't adopt that tone. Let's come to business. What is it you want?

SEREBRIAKOV: ... I have invited you here, ladies and gentlemen, to inform you that the Inspector General is coming to visit us.

It is the jest for which we have been waiting, and harks back to Gogol's comedy, *The Government Inspector*. No one laughs. They gaze at him blankly.

SEREBRIAKOV: But, joking apart ... I have called you together, my friends, to ask your help and advice ... I'm an academic, bookish man, and I've never had anything to do with practical life ... I'm an old and ailing man, and I think it's high time to settle the matter of my property in so far as it concerns my family. My own life is over now, I'm not thinking of myself. But I have a young wife and an unmarried daughter. [*A pause.*] It is impossible for me to go on living in the country. We are not made for country life. But to live in town on the income we are receiving from this estate is also impossible. Suppose we sold the forest – that would be an exceptional measure which could not be repeated every year. We must find ways which will guarantee us a permanent, more or less definite income. One such measure has occurred to me, and I would like to submit it for your consideration . . . Our estate yields on the average not more than two per cent on its capital value. I suggest we sell it. [*There is a general gasp of disbelief and disapproval from all save Yeliena, who is deep in a daydream.*] If we invest the money in suitable securities . . . we might even have a few thousand roubles to spare which would enable us to buy a small villa in Finland.

VOINITSKY: . . . Surely I haven't been hearing correctly. Say that again.

SEREBRIAKOV: I suggest we sell the estate.

VOINITSKY: . . . And where do you propose I should go – with my old mother and Sonia here?

SEREBRIAKOV: . . . We can't do everything at once.

VOINITSKY: [*becoming heavily sarcastic*] . . . It looks as though I must have been incredibly stupid all this time. Until now I've been foolish enough to believe that this estate belonged to Sonia . . .

SEREBRIAKOV: Yes, the estate belongs to Sonia. Who's disputing it? Without Sonia's consent I shall not venture to sell it. Besides [*he wags a finger*], I am suggesting that this should be done for Sonia's benefit.

VOINITSKY: It's inconceivable, inconceivable! Either I've gone out of my mind, or – or . . .

The scene builds up to Vanya's pistol shots, which we have already examined.

In Act IV matters and man are sorted, hastily, and the rondo Voinitsky arrives at its *ritornello*.

When the curtain rises we are in Vanya's combined office and bedroom. The good neighbour Teleyeghin is holding the skeins of wool which the old nurse, Marina, is winding, and as she winds they act for us as a Greek chorus:

TELYEGHIN: Hurry up, Marina Timofyeevna. They'll soon be calling us to say good-bye. They've ordered the horses to be brought round . . . They're going to Harkov. Going to live there.

MARINA: That will be much better.

TELYEGHIN: They've had a fright. Yeliena Andryeevna keeps saying: 'I won't stay here another hour – Let's get away – Let's get away' . . . It seems they're not ordained to live here, Marina Timofyeevna. They're not ordained to – Such is the will of Providence.

MARINA: It's better so. The row they made this morning – and shooting, too – a regular disgrace! . . . What a sight for my old eyes! [*A pause.*] We'll be living again as we used to – in the old way. Morning tea soon after seven, dinner at twelve, and in the evening we'll sit down to supper. Everything as it should be, just like other people – like Christians. [*With a sigh.*] It's a long time since I tasted noodles, sinner that I am!

TELYEGHIN: . . . As I was walking through the village this morning, the shopkeeper shouted after me: 'Hey, you scrounger – living on other people, you are!' I felt so hurt!

MARINA: . . . We all live on God.

For Vanya it is a bitter moment. He is outside the house with Dr Astrov.

VOINITSKY: To have made such a fool of myself – firing twice and missing both times! I shall never forgive myself for that!

And now we see that, as so often in Chekhov, and in this play, our laughter has been balanced on a tear, for a little later he says:

VOINITSKY: [*covers his face with his hands*] I feel so ashamed. If you only knew how ashamed I feel! This acute sense of shame – it's worse than any pain! ... What am I to do? What am I to do? ... [*pleading with the doctor*] Give me something! Oh my God! I'm forty-seven. If I live to be sixty, I've got another thirteen years ... How am I to get through those thirteen years? ... How shall I fill in the time?

Astrov has found out that Vanya has taken a phial of morphine from his bag. He knows that he must take it from the neurotic 'two-and-twenty misfortunes'. Sonia, who is to stay on with Vanya to run the estate, appeals to her uncle:

SONIA: Uncle Vanya, did you take the morphia? [*A pause.*] Give it back. Why do you frighten us like this? [*With tenderness.*] Give it back, Uncle Vanya! I dare say I'm just as unhappy as you are, but I don't despair all the same. I bear it, and I shall continue to bear it till my life comes to its natural end. – You must bear it, too. [*A pause.*] ... My dear, kind uncle – give it up, dear! [*Weeps.*] You're so good, I know you'll feel sorry for us and give it back. You'll have to bear it, Uncle! You must bear it!

Vanya surrenders the bottle to Astrov.

VOINITSKY: Here, take it! [*To Sonia.*] But we must start work at once, we must start doing something, or else I can't – I can't . . .

SONIA: Yes, yes, work. As soon as we've seen the others off, we'll settle down to work – We've been neglecting everything.

It is a scene of leave-taking – one of the two most beautiful of such scenes in all Chekhov. Yeliena takes leave of Astrov:

YELIENA: . . . We shall never see each other again, and so why should I conceal it? – you did turn my head a little . . . Think well of me.

ASTROV: It is strange somehow – Here we've known one another and all at once for some reason – we shall never see each other again. That's the way with everything in this world – While there's no one here – before Uncle Vanya comes in with a bunch of flowers, allow me – to kiss you – good-bye . . .

YELIENA: . . . For once in my life! [*Embraces him impulsively*]

The professor takes leave of Vanya:

SEREBRIAKOV: Let us let bygones be bygones . . . I gladly accept your apologies and I ask you to forgive me too. Good-bye! (*He and* VOINITSKY *embrace and kiss each other three times.*]

VOINITSKY: You'll be receiving the same amount as before, regularly. Everything shall be as it was before.

SEREBRIAKOV: [*to the company at large*] . . . Permit an old man to add one thing to his farewell greetings: you must try to do real work, my friends, yes, real work!

The last adieu has been said. The old house has seemed to sigh with relief and settle back on its haunches as the sound of the bells of the station-waggon fade into the distance.

ASTROV: They've gone. The professor's glad, that's certain. Wild horses won't drag him back.

This may be Astrov's view, but there could be another opinion, and we shall hear it before we take leave of the idiosyncratic but lovable Voinitskys.

The old nurse comes in and hobbles across the room.

MARINA: They've gone [*Sits down in an easy chair and knits a stocking.*]

SONIA: [*comes in wiping her eyes*] They've gone. God grant them a safe journey. [*Pause.*] Well, Uncle Vanya, let's start doing something.

VOINITSKY: Work, work . . .

SONIA: It's a long, long time since we sat at this table, just the two of us. [*she lights the lamp*]

MARIA VASSILIEVNA: [*coming slowly in*] Gone! [*Sits down and becomes absorbed in reading.*]

Astrov throws back a glass of vodka and departs: Sonia follows him with a lighted candle, then returns tearfully.

MARINA: He's gone.

VOINITSKY: [*to Sonia*] My child, there's such a weight on my heart! Oh, if only you knew how my heart aches!

And thus to the play's quiet close:

SONIA: ... We must go on living! We shall go on living, Uncle Vanya! We shall live through a long, long succession of days and tedious evenings. We shall patiently suffer the trials which Fate imposes on us; we shall work for others, now and [*her gaze travels to the old nurse*] in our old age . . . When our time comes we shall die, submissively, and over there, beyond the grave, we shall say that we've suffered, that we've wept, that we've had a bitter life, and God will take pity on us. And then, Uncle dear, we shall both begin to know a life that is bright and beautiful, and lovely. We shall rejoice and look back at these troubles of ours with tender feelings, with a smile – and we shall have rest. I believe it, Uncle, I believe it fervently, passionately – [*Kneels before him and lays her head on his hands, then in a tired voice.*] We shall have rest! . . . We shall have rest! We shall hear the angels, we shall see all the heavens covered with stars like diamonds, we shall see all earthly evil, all our sufferings swept away by the grace which will fill the whole world, and our life will become peaceful, gentle, and sweet as a caress. I believe it, I believe it – [*Wipes his eyes with her handkerchief.*] Poor, poor Uncle Vanya, you're crying. You've had no joy in your life, but wait, Uncle Vanya, wait – We shall rest – We shall rest! [*The watchman taps.*] We shall rest!

and Chekhov's instruction is:

THE CURTAIN DROPS SLOWLY

'Every happy family resembles one another,' wrote Tolstoy, 'every unhappy family is unhappy in its own way.'

Within the canon Chekhov's families appear to bear Tolstoy out in this. In *The Seagull, Uncle Vanya, The Three Sisters* and *The Cherry Orchard* we certainly find four unhappy families, but their collective state of soul varies. In *The Seagull* the Trepliovs are the most passionately neurasthenic. The Voinitskys in *Uncle Vanya* are the most violent. In *The Three Sisters* the Family Prozorov are the saddest because for them fate can find no happy ending. In *The Cherry Orchard* the Ranyevskis, at the end of their resources, depend on finance which is at a low ebb, and like the three sisters Prozorov their chiaroscuro is the more underlined by the highlights of sudden merriment and heart's ease that light up the scene by flashes as though by summer lightning.

Once I squandered three weeks, in the form of a short story, trying to sort out what happened to Uncle Vanya and his difficult family after the end of the play. In spite of their protestations on parting I in no way feel that the end of their story coincided with the slow falling of the curtain in the last act. It seemed to me that all those 'They've gones' which thread the play's final moments will surely be followed, next summer by 'They are back! ... They are back!' For one thing, come the summer that perpetual and petulant invalid, the professor, and his lambent young wife will have overspent their slender money in the somewhat dusty delights of Harkov or some other provincial town. The choice that Liubov Ranyevskaia could not bring herself to face now confronts the Family Voinitsky – to sell or not to sell.

Moreover they have their private problems. Yeliena has, for the first time, tasted the sweets of having fallen, however little, in love (for we cannot believe that the love she bore her infuriating husband was much more than that which a dutiful daughter owes her sick father, and also, perhaps, due to a certain enjoyment in her social improvement in the eyes of the world for having become the wife of a professor). So, newly returned from her near-amorous encounter with Astrov, the tired volcano, she falls head over heels in love with the first penniless *poseur* she meets, so echoing the fate of Madame Ranyevskaia; in fact Yeliena will have become what we in our own age would flippantly call the poor man's Ranyevskaia. She will have become recklessly extravagant both in her wardrobe of costly clothes and flimsy underclothes and in the even costlier matter of constantly saving her spendthrift provincial lover from his debtors. Her position in society is maintained only through her boring yet demanding marriage.

Astrov, the man of trees, is to her a tale that is over. Her summer loving disintegrated in the last mists of that autumn. She will be concerned about Astrov's frame of mind – will he expect them to take up their romance where they had left it – on a passionate kiss? She will be profoundly disturbed. Yet if he has changed it will be a blow to her self-conceit.

Vanya and Sonia will be the constant factor in the scenes of the second summer, both sighing for the wrong loved one and doomed to be for ever unfulfilled.

Astrov will be as wary of Yeliena, did she but know, as she of him. He has returned to his first love, his trees, and does not want his heart to pound again in this, his carpet-slipper time of life. He is accustomed to the feeling of guilt that springs from his practice of medicine and will not want to add to it by an exhausting marriage to a spoilt young wife – for by now the professor will have died suddenly, probably in the middle of an idiotic wrangle with Vanya, leaving Yeliena penniless and insecure. It all seems very bleak as I recount it, without benefit of the constant interplay of sun and shadow that is Chekhov's own gift to his sad families.

If Chekhov did not like the plays of Ibsen (as we have seen, he thought Ibsen 'dry, cold, a man of reason') Tolstoy did not like the work of Chekhov. The courtship of the married Yeliena by both Vanya and Astrov so outraged Tolstoy that he insulted one of the actors after a performance, we are told. On another occasion, when discussing *Uncle Vanya* with Chekhov, he said: 'You know that I cannot bear Shakespeare? Well, your plays are even worse than his.'

Stanislavski, however, writing *My Life in Art*, perceived the total strength of Chekhov's mature plays. These are plays written on the simplest themes, he says, which in themselves are not interesting. But they are permeated by that which is eternal. Chekhov is a writer of such plays: 'Read him in the kitchen of life and you will find nothing in him but the simple plot' – such as today we designate as a non-plot – 'mosquitoes, crickets, boredom, grey little people whose lives are being eaten away by ennui. But,' writes Stanislavski, 'take him where art soars and you will feel in the everyday plots of his plays the eternal longings of man for happiness, his strivings upwards, the true aroma of Russian poetry, in no smaller measure than it is felt in Turgenev' – Turgenev, who was both Chekhov's rival and his idol.

The Three Sisters

Why do you not try to write a play? It gives you exactly the same feeling as when for the first time you creep into an unwarmed bed on a cold night, according to Chekhov in a letter to a friend. Yet thinking about Chekhov's plays, discussing them with actors and directors, even writing about them, is one of the particular pleasures of a drama critic's peculiar trade. Writing about *The Three Sisters* is, however, the most difficult task in a commentary of the plays within the canon. It is not unlike prodding a jelly with a spoon – prod it as you will it returns to its original mystery. Dramatically the play has an amorphous shape that does not make for clear definition.

Yet this play, devoid of commonplace over-emphasis, as are all Chekhov's mature plays, shows the depths beneath the depths common to all humanity. As a masterpiece of writing for the stage it stands without flaw or blemish. As Maurice Baring pointed out, Chekhov never underlines his effects, never nudges the reader's elbow.

We could do worse than take a fleeting look at the people in the play.

Life has left three sisters, Olga, Masha and Irena, the daughters of a colonel, in the small provincial town where he died. Moscow, where they were born, though they have never returned to it, is their Jerusalem, flowing with milk and honey and husbands, bright with balls and concerts, with sophistication and ease. One suspects however that they would be dreadfully disappointed if the Family Prozorov uprooted itself to go there. But this is a play by Chekhov, so there is no risk of their actually arriving, one snowy day.

In their dull provincial town is a garrison. High-spirited young officers frequent the family home. Among them is a Baron Toozenbach, a lieutenant about to leave the army to look after his local brickyard ('I've never done a stroke of work in my life. I was born in Petersburg, an unfriendly, idle city – born into a family where work and worries were simply unknown . . .').

Toozenbach is in love with Irena, the youngest of the three sisters:

IRENA: What lovely weather it is today! Really, I don't know why there's such joy in my heart. I remembered this morning that it was my Saint's day, and suddenly I felt so happy, and I thought of the time when we were children, and Mother was still alive. And then such wonderful thoughts came to me, such wonderful stirring thoughts!

Colonel Vershinin, the commander of the battery, a lemon-tea philosopher trailing an unhappy marriage, is newly arrived in town. He loses no time in falling in love with Masha, the middle sister. Chekhov makes this tea-glass philosopher Vershinin the speaker of the prediction that is in all four of the great plays:

VERSHININ: . . . It may well be that in time to come the life we
live today will seem strange and uncomfortable and stupid
and not too clean, either, and perhaps even wicked . . .

TOOZENBACH: Who can tell? It's just as possible that future
generations will think that we lived our lives on a very high
plane and remember us with respect. After all, we no longer
have tortures and public executions . . . though there's still
a great deal of suffering!

Masha, who later complains that to know three languages in a
town like theirs is an unnecessary luxury ('In fact, not even a
luxury, but just a sort of useless encumbrance . . . rather like
having a sixth finger on your hand . . .'), is married to a patient
but particularly foolish schoolteacher, Koolyahin. It is interesting to find that whenever Chekhov wrote about
schoolteachers he saw them as foolish and patient. He was ap-
palled by their poverty-stricken lives and the lack of proper
respect extended to them and devoted much of his time and
what money he could spare to building up their social status:

KOOLYGHIN: . . . We shall have to roll up the carpets and put
them away till the winter. – We must remember to put
some naphthaline on them, or Persian powder. – The
Romans enjoyed good health because they knew how to
work *and* how to rest. They had *mens sana in corpore sano* . . . ,
Masha loves me. My wife loves me. Yes, and the curtains
will have to be put away with the carpets, too . . .

How Chekhov manages to create bores without boring the
audience is a part of the magic known only to him.

Masha is, in fact, thoroughly bored with her dull husband, his
pathetic jokes and the whole of the Prozorov scene, from which
she can see no escape. Masha falls in love all too easily with the
somewhat seedy Don Juan, Vershinin.

The third and eldest sister, Olga, is a schoolteacher, too. One of nature's spinsters, she takes refuge in headaches:

OLGA: ... I suppose I must get this continual headache because I have to go to school every day and go on teaching right into the evening. I seem to have the thoughts of someone quite old. I've been feeling as though my strength and youth were running out of me drop by drop, day after day ... I just have one longing and it seems to grow stronger and stronger.

IRENA: If only we could go back to Moscow! ... finish with our life here, and go back to Moscow.

OLGA: Yes, Moscow! ...

The sisters have a brother, Andrey: weak, a gambler, a spoiled academic who has now become stuck in a dreary council office, where the only alleviations to his seedy lot are cards and drink:

ANDREY: I won't play cards tonight, I'll just sit and watch. I'm not feeling too well. – What ought I to do for this breathlessness, Ivan Romanych?

CHEBUTYKIN: [an aged army doctor] Why ask me, dear boy? I can't remember – I simply don't know.

Andrey is engaged and subsequently marries a vulgar little woman of whom his sisters strongly disapprove:

OLGA: [Alarmed, dropping her voice.] You've got a green belt on! My dear, that's surely a mistake!

NATASHA: Why, is it a bad omen, or what?

OLGA: No, but it just doesn't go with your dress – it looks so strange.

Before we meet her Masha, too, has been criticizing her:

MASHA: The way she dresses herself is awful! It's not that her clothes are just ugly and old-fashioned, they're simply pathetic. She'll put on some weird-looking, bright yellow skirt with a crude sort of fringe affair, and then a red blouse to go with it. And her cheeks look as though they've been scrubbed, they are so shiny . . . I heard yesterday that she's going to get married to Protopopov, the chairman of the local council. I thought it was an excellent idea.

Among the officers is a saturnine captain, Soliony, who is to play a dark role in the life of Irena and Toozenbach. A bitter man whose nerves are always at stretch, he is egged on by them to pick a quarrel whenever the opportunity occurs.

There, with a spattering of young officers, you have them all. And, like a near-holy halo surrounding the sisters' every mood, is the presence of Moscow as they have dreamed it, almost a character in its own right, threading the sisters' conversation like a chime of bells from a city of belfries. 'Moscow! Moscow! Moscow!' cries Irena, with a mounting intensity, as the curtain falls on the second act. The three sisters and their fate are to be the content of Chekhov's most poignant play.

A letter from Yalta sent to A. L. Vishnevsky, an actor, heralded *The Three Sisters:*

Yalta, August 5, 1900
I am writing the play, have already written a great deal of it, but as long as I am not in Moscow I can form no judgment about the play. Perhaps what I am turning out is not a play but wearisome Crimean fiddle-faddle. It is called *Three Sisters* . . . for you I am working on the role of a high school inspector, husband of one of the sisters. You will be wearing your uniform and will have a decoration on a ribbon around your neck.

Should the play not go into production this season I will rework it next season.

This was followed by a groan for privacy, for time to let concentration grow into a habit. On 18 August 1900 he wrote to Olga Knipper from Yalta:

My sweet little pet,
... I am being hindered, cruelly, vilely and basely hindered. The play is complete in my head, has taken form from where my imagination left off and is pleading to be set onto paper, but hardly do I place a sheet of paper in front of me than the door opens and some ugly mug intrudes. I don't know how it is going to turn out, but the start is not bad, pretty smooth, I think.

But by September the habit of following and pondering the play began to bear fruit and on the fifth he was writing once again to Olga Knipper:

Yalta, September 5, 1900

My darling, my angel,
... All this time I've been poring over my play, meditating rather than writing, yet it seemed to me that I was busy with real work and I had no mind for letters. I am writing the play but I am not hurrying with it, and it is very possible that I shall leave for Moscow without having finished it. There are a great many characters, it is crowded, I'm afraid it will turn out obscure or pale, and so I think it may be better to put it off till next season. By the way, only *Ivanov* I allowed to be produced at Korsh's immediately after writing it. All the other plays I kept by me for a long time, waiting for Nemirovich-Danchenko, and thus I had a chance to make all kinds of corrections.

Three days later an incensed note went buzzing angrily off to Olga Knipper:

> *September 8, 1900, Yalta*
>
> ... Is Gorki writing a play or isn't he? Whence the note in *News of the Day* about the title *The Three Sisters* not being appropriate? What stuff and nonsense! Perhaps it isn't suitable, but I have no intention of changing it.

In the middle of October Chekhov, sure of a colleague and fellow-playwright's understanding, wrote to Maxim Gorki:

> *October 16, 1900, Yalta*
>
> My dear Alexei Maximovich,
>
> ... Writing *The Three Sisters* was terribly hard work. It has three heroines, you know, each one has to be a special type, and all three of them are a general's daughters! The action takes place in a provincial city, on the order of Perm, and the surroundings are military, an artillery unit.

But by November distrust and doubt had set in, as we see in his letter to V. F. Kommisarjevskaya:

> *Moscow, November 13, 1900*
>
> ... *Three Sisters* are already finished, but their future, their immediate future, at least – is veiled from me by the murk of uncertainty. The play has turned out to be boring, long-drawn-out, awkward – awkward, I say, since it has four female leads, for instance, and its mood I am told, is gloomier than gloom.
>
> It would prove very, very little to the liking of your artists if I were to send it to the Alexandrinsky Theatre, but, come what may, send the play to you I will. Read it and decide whether it is worth while to take it along on your tour this

summer. It is now being read in the Art Theatre (there is only one copy, no more) ...

By the middle of December courage had returned to Chekhov and he was writing to Olga Knipper from Nice, where he had gone for his health:

Nice, December 17, 1900

... Yesterday sent Act III of play to Moscow, and tomorrow will send Act IV. In III I changed only a little here and there, but in IV I went in for drastic changes. I fattened up your part a lot (You are supposed to say 'Thank you ...') And you, in return, write me how the rehearsals are going, what's what and how things are – write everything ...

Nine days later he wrote again to her:

Nice, December 26, 1900

... Write how the rehearsals are going, which act you have reached ... In general, how is the work going: would it not be better to postpone the play till next season?

Write, or I'll smash you to pieces.

The New Year came and with it another plea to Olga Knipper for news of his play:

Nice, January 2, 1901

... Do describe at least one rehearsal of *Three Sisters*. Ought anything to be put in or taken out? Are you acting well, my darling? Oh, mind now! Don't make a mournful face in a single act. Angry, yes, but not mournful. People who carry grief in their hearts a long time and are used to it only whistle and often sink into thought. So you may often be thoughtful on the stage during conversations. Do you understand? ...

On the same day Chekhov wrote to Stanislavski:

January 2, 1901, Nice

... As to that old play, *The Three Sisters*, reading it at the Countess' [Tolstoy] evening party is absolutely forbidden under any circumstances. For God's sake, I beg of you, don't read it ... Otherwise you will cause me a great deal of anguish.

... I have made a great many changes. You tell me that in Act III, when Natasha makes the rounds of the house at night, she extinguishes the lights and looks for evil-doers under the furniture. But it seems to me it would be preferable to have her walk across the stage in a straight line without looking at anything or anyone, *à la* Lady Macbeth, with a candle – that way the scene would be shorter and more bloodcurdling.

A few days later that poignant longing for news – any news – of his play can again be seen in his letter to Olga Knipper:

Nice, January 11, 1901

... Write, dog! Auburn-haired dog! Not to write to me – this is so mean of you! If at least you wrote me what is happening to *Three Sisters*. You haven't yet written me anything about the play, absolutely nothing ...

Write, darling, I implore you.

Still writing from his Mediterranean exile, Chekhov explained a couple of points in the text for a member of the cast, Joasaph Tikhomirov:

January 14, 1901, Nice

... Here are the answers to your questions:

1. Irena does not know that Toozenbach is having a duel, but surmises that something went wrong that may have grave, not to say tragic, consequences. And when a woman guesses, she says, 'I knew it, I knew it.'

2. Chebutykin only sings the words, 'Would it not please

you to accept this date . . .' These are words from an operetta which was given some time ago at the Hermitage ... Chebutykin must not sing anything else or his exit will be too prolonged.

... Nobody writes me anything about the play; Nemirovich-Danchenko never said a word about it when he was here and it seemed to me it bored him and wouldn't be successful. Your letter . . . helped to dispel my melancholy.

And on 15 January he sent a suggestion to Stanislavski which the Moscow Art Theatre adopted and which has been used in every production I have seen since:

January 15, 1901, Nice
. . . Of course you are a thousand times right, it wouldn't do at all to show Toozenbach's body. I myself felt it when I wrote the play and spoke to you of it . . . That the finale reminds one of *Uncle Vanya* [Oh, Chekhov, dramatist of farewells!] is a minor evil. *Uncle Vanya* happens to be my own play, and not someone else's and when you are reminiscent of yourself in your works, people will say that is the way it should be . . .

By 26 January 1901 Chekhov showed unconsciously what a model author he had grown to be:

Yalta, January 26, 1901
Dear Mariya Fyodorovna [M. F. Andreyeva],
. . . You write that during my last visit I pained you because I seemed afraid to speak frankly with you about *Three Sisters* . . . God forbid! I was not afraid to speak frankly with you, I was afraid of hindering you and on purpose I tried to hold my peace, and as far as possible restrain myself, precisely in order not to interfere with your work. If I had remained in Moscow, perhaps after the tenth rehearsal I would have made some remarks, and those only about details. They

1 The Chekhov family outside their home in Moscow

2 (*below left*) Anton Chekhov and his wife, Olga Knipper, an actress with the Moscow Arts Theatre

3 (*below right*) Chekhov with his mother (seated) and sister, Maria (left) and Olga Knipper in 1901

5 (right) Chekhov with the cast of
The Seagull, 1898

4 (above) The Moscow Arts Theatre

6 (right) A scene from the original
production of *The Seagull* at Moscow
Arts Theatre, 1898

7 The original production of *Uncle Vanya*, 1899 at Moscow with Olga Knipper as Yeliena Andreyeevna and Stanislavski, the famous Russian actor, as Astrov, 1899

9 (*above*) The climax of Act III of
The Cherry Orchard at Moscow, 1904

8 The original production of *The
Three Sisters* at Moscow, 1901

10 John Gielgud as Toozenbach and Beatrix Thomson as Irena in the 1926 production of *The Three Sisters* at Barnes

11 Stephen Haggart as Trepliov and Peggy Ashcroft as Nina in the 1936 production of *The Seagull* at the New Theatre

12 From left to right: Ralph Richardson, Lawrence Olivier, Margaret Leighton and Joyce Redman in the 1945 production of *Uncle Vanya* at the New Theatre

13 John Gielgud as Gaev, Peggy Ashcroft as Madame Ranyevskaia and Dorothy Tutin as Varia in the Royal Shakespeare Company's production of *The Cherry Orchard* at Stratford, 1961

write me from Moscow that you are excellent in *Three Sisters* [she played Irena], that you play simply marvellously, and I am glad, very glad . . .

On 31 January 1901 *The Three Sisters* opened in Moscow and after a short season there went to St Petersburg, where it was not well received. Chekhov wrote from Yalta to comfort his beloved Olga:

March 1, 1901, Yalta

My dear one,
Don't read the newspapers, don't read anything, or you will pine away altogether. Here is some sound advice for future reference: heed the words of your old holy hermit. Certainly I told you . . . that things wouldn't go well in St Petersburg – and you should have listened to me. At any rate, your theatre will never again visit the place – thank God.

Personally I am giving up the theatre entirely, and will never write again for it. It is possible to write for the stage in Germany, in Sweden, even in Spain, but not in Russia, where dramatic authors are not respected, are kicked around and are forgiven neither their successes nor their failures. You are being abused now for the first time in your life, which accounts your sensitiveness, but it will pass away with time, and you'll get used to such treatment . . .

In May, 1901, Chekhov married Olga Knipper 'secretly'. When they told his mother and sister, predictably they did not approve and a certain amount of sniping and feuding took place. In March 1902 Olga suffered a miscarriage, which cut Chekhov to the quick. But the first week in September he was writing:

September 6, 1902, Yalta

My little crocodile, my unusual wife,

... Fomin came to see me; he delivers public lectures on *The Three Sisters* and *Three of Us* (by Chekhov and Gorki). He is an honest, high-minded, but obviously not very bright little gentleman.

In the first week in November, when *The Three Sisters* was given at the New Moscow Art Theatre, Chekhov wrote to Leopold Sulerzhitsky from that city:

November 5, 1902, Moscow

The new theatre is very fine; spacious, bright, no cheap, glaring luxury. The acting remains as ever ... good ... Meierhold is not missed; Kachalov substitutes for him in *The Three Sisters* and turns in a magnificent performance ...

Chekhov sent *The Three Sisters* to the Moscow Art Theatre act by act, as though tearing it out of himself, but he arrived in Moscow with Act IV personally. Stanislavski gives a description of the author's read-through in *My Life in Art*:

As was our custom, a large table was placed in the foyer of the theatre and covered with cloth, and we all sat down around it, the author and the stage directors in the centre. The atmosphere was triumphant and uplifted. All the members of the company, the ushers, some of the stage-hands and even a tailor or two were present. The author was apparently excited ... Now and then he would leap from his chair and walk about, especially at those moments when the conversation ... took a false or unpleasant direction. After the reading of the play, some of us ... called it a drama and others even a tragedy, without noticing that these definitions amazed Chekhov . . .

. . . he had written a happy comedy and all of us had considered the play a tragedy and even wept over it . . . Chekhov thought that the play had been misunderstood and that it was already a failure . . .

We worked with spirit. We rehearsed the play, everything was clear, comprehensive, true, but the play did not live; it was hollow, it seemed tiresome and long. There was something missing. How torturing it is to seek this something without knowing what it is. [What torture indeed!] . . . Yet . . . we felt that there were elements that augured great success, that everything with the exception of that little something was present . . . We met daily, we rehearsed to a point of despair, we parted company, and next day we would meet again and reach despair once more.

. . . 'We are dragging the thing out . . .' [suggested a member of the company]. 'We must lift the tone and play in quick tempo' . . .

The men of Chekhov do not bathe, as we did at that time, in their own sorrow. Just the opposite; they, like Chekhov himself, seek life, joy, laughter, courage. The men and women of Chekhov want to live and not to die . . . It is not their fault that Russian life kills initiative . . .

One of the happiest things about my ponderings on Chekhov, I have found, is the point at which, like the fictional Christopher Isherwood in *Goodbye to Berlin,* I am a camera, wheeling round the masterpiece and about the people in the play, pausing here and there for a close-up and watching fate change the patterns of their lot. Stripping *The Three Sisters* as though I were a storm, and the characters in the play trees in the grip of a remorseless winter, I find that clean lines emerge, and a strict graph appears. The sisters are entertaining the officers of the garrison. They long to go to Moscow. We know that they never will. The soldiers depart, leaving them planted in their empty lives, now emptier than ever. The *rondo* of fate has been achieved.

Once, with time on my hands (it can happen to anyone once or twice in a professional lifetime), I spent an hour or so imagining what would happen if in fact the Prozorovs ever did get to Moscow, only to come up with the insistent certainty that they would hate it. The good Muscovites would find them frumpish and old fashioned. No one would call to take them to balls, the ballet, concerts. The one success in the little parcel of prudes from Perm, or wherever (Chekhov points to the similarity of the small provincial town to Perm in a stage direction), would be the vulgar sister-in-law, Natasha, who would laugh her brassy laugh and dress unsuitably but in bright colours, and would not be too particular where or with whom she went on sleigh-rides.

But back to Chekhov.

How Ibsen might have envied his opening to *The Three Sisters*, had the stroke that paralysed his last three years fallen after he had seen or read it, though his health was already failing in 1900 and Chekhov's play was first produced on 31 January 1901. Never can a play's end have been written more conclusively in its beginning.

The play opens in the drawing-room in the Prozorovs' house. Olga, wearing 'the regulation dark-blue dress of a secondary school mistress', is correcting exercise books. Masha is in black and usually we meet her in an ill-tempered hunch on a *chaise-longue*. Irena, in white, stands lost in thought:

OLGA: It's exactly a year ago that Father died, isn't it? This very day, the fifth of May – your Saint's day, Irena. I remember it was very cold and it was snowing. I felt then as if I should never survive his death; and you had fainted and were lying quite still, as if you were dead. And now – a year's gone by, and we talk of it so easily. You're wearing white, and your face is positively radiant . . . [*A clock strikes twelve.*] The clock struck twelve then, too. [*A pause.*] I remember when Father was being taken to the cemetery there was a military band, and a salute with rifle fire. That was because he was a general, in command of a brigade. And yet there weren't many people at the funeral. Of course, it was raining hard, raining and snowing . . . It's so warm today that we can keep the windows wide open, and yet there aren't any leaves showing on the birch trees. Father was made a brigadier eleven years ago, and then he left Moscow and took us with him. I remember so well how everything in Moscow was in blossom by now, everything was soaked in sunlight and warmth. Eleven years have gone by, yet I remember everything about it, as if we'd only left yesterday. Oh, Heavens! When I woke up this morning and saw this flood of sunshine, . . . I felt so moved and so happy! I felt such a longing to get back home to Moscow! . . . Day after day, all these four years that I've been working at the school – I just have one longing and it seems to grow stronger and stronger –

IRENA: If only we could go back to Moscow! Sell the house, finish with our life here, and go back to Moscow.

OLGA: Yes, Moscow! As soon as we possibly can.

IRENA: . . . The only problem is our poor Masha.

OLGA: Masha can come and stay the whole summer with us every year in Moscow.

IRENA: Everything will settle itself, with God's help.

But as we are to find out, the Almighty was not, in the event, in a co-operative mood.

Olga is the eldest of the sisters. It comes as a shock when we learn how young she is:

OLGA: [*to Irena*] You're so lovely today, you really do look most attractive. Masha looks pretty today, too. Andrey could be good-looking, but he's grown so stout. It doesn't suit him. As for me, I've just aged and grown a lot thinner. I suppose it's through getting so irritated with the girls at school. But today I'm at home, I'm free, and my headache's gone, and I feel much younger than I did yesterday. I'm only twenty-eight, after all.

Olga goes on to expose the root of the matter:

I suppose everything that God wills must be right and good, but I can't help thinking sometimes that if I'd got married and stayed at home, it would have been a better thing for me. [*A pause.*] I would have been very fond of my husband.

In Act III she returns to the theme of marriage while the shadow thrown by the fire in the township leaps as though it would eat the bedroom walls:

IRENA: [*trying to control herself*] Oh, I'm so miserable! – I can't work, I won't work! I've had enough of it, enough! . . . I'm twenty-three years old, I've been working all this time, and I feel as if my brain's dried up. I know I've got thinner and uglier and older . . . And the time is passing – and I feel as if I'm moving away from any hope of a genuine, fine life, I'm moving further and further away and sinking into a kind of abyss . . .
OLGA: Darling, let me tell you something – I just want to speak as your sister, as your friend . . . Why don't you marry the Baron (Toozenbach)? [*Irena weeps*] After all, you do respect him . . . It's true, he's not good-looking, but he's

such a decent, clean-minded sort of man. – After all, one doesn't marry for love, but to fulfil a duty. At least, I think so . . . I'd marry anyone that proposed to me, as long as he was a decent man. I'd even marry an old man.

IRENA: [*disconsolate*] I've been waiting all this time, imagining that we'd be moving to Moscow, and I'd meet the man I'm meant for there. I've dreamt about him and I've loved him in my dreams – But it's all turned out to be non-sense – nonsense . . .

Marriage and Moscow – they are synonymous in Irena's imagination. Neither she nor Olga has been turned from the golden dream by the day-to-day spectacle of Masha's dull marriage.

In this scene of the red glow of devastation both Masha and Andrey ('Andrey could be good-looking, but he's grown so stout. It doesn't suit him') have a confession to make and it spills out of them. It has been a scene of the utmost confusion. Friends have taken refuge in the house. Clothes have been sorted and sent to the victims of the fire. Natasha has railed at the sisters' old nanny, Uncle Chebutykin has got drunk, Koolyghin has been up searching for his wife, who has been with Vershinin:

VERSHININ: And when my little girls were standing in the doorway with nothing on but their night clothes, and the street was red with the glow of the fire and full of terrifying noises, it struck me that the same sort of thing used to happen years ago . . . And before very long, say, in another two or three hundred years, people may be looking at our present life . . . with horror and scorn.

Fire or no, Chekhov is away with Vershinin on his favourite theme: ('Oh, what a great life it'll be then, what a life!') and on such a night as this, the lovable Prozorovs launch themselves four-fold into confidences of the utmost concern to them and to us, and, were they not to do so, they would not be the Prozorovs. First Masha, unrepentant, spoilt wife. Then Andrey, spoiled professor:

MASHA: My dear sisters, I've got something to confess to you. [*The flames leap and glow.*] I must get some relief, I feel the need of it in my heart. I'll confess it to you two alone . . . I can't keep silent any more. I'm in love, in love . . . I love Vershinin.

OLGA: [*goes behind her screen*] Don't say it. I don't want to hear it.

MASHA: Well, what's to be done? I thought he was strange at first, then I started to pity him – then I began to love him [a Muscovite Desdemona?] – love everything about him – his voice, his talk, his misfortunes [including a wife who threatens suicide], his two little girls.

OLGA: . . . You can say any nonsense you like, I'm not listening.

MASHA: . . . He loves me, too. It's all rather frightening, isn't it? Not a good thing, is it? [*Takes Irena by the hand.*] . . . How are we going to live through the rest of our lives? What's going to become of us?

And now Andrey, a weak man with pepper in his soul, entirely ruled by his vulgar little pigeon, Natasha; his only escape, gambling.

ANDREY: What a terrific fire! . . . Why don't you say anything, Olia? . . . sulking like this for no reason whatever – You here, Masha? And Irena's here, too? That's excellent! We can talk it over then, frankly and once for all. What have you got against me? What is it?

Now Olga says the most sensible thing that has been said all night:

OLGA: Drop it, now, Andriusha. Let's talk it over tomorrow. [*Agitated.*] What a dreadful night!

ANDREY: . . . I'm asking you quite calmly, what have you got against me? Tell me frankly.

Vershinin's voice is heard off-stage singing a snatch of song – it's a signal. Masha sings an answering snatch. She gets up to go, kisses her two sisters:

MASHA: . . . Sleep well – Good-bye, Andrey. I should leave them now, they're tired – Talk it over tomorrow. [*She goes to join Vershinin.*]

But Andrey is already in full spate:

ANDREY: . . . First of all, you've got something against my wife, against Natasha. I've always been conscious of it from the day we got married. Natasha is a fine woman, she's honest and straightforward and high-principled . . .

She is also flamboyant, of the earth, earthy, and grabbing.

ANDREY: . . . Secondly, you seem to be annoyed with me for not making myself a professor . . . But I'm working in the Central Office, I'm a member of the County Council, and I feel my service there is just as fine and valuable as any academic work I might do . . . Thirdly – there's something else I must tell you – I know I mortgaged the house without asking your permission – that was wrong, I admit it, and I ask you to forgive me – I was driven to it by my debts – I'm in debt for about thirty-five thousand roubles . . .

There is a pause through which Koolyghin can be heard calling through the door:

KOOLYGHIN: Is Masha there? She's not there? [*Alarmed.*] Where can she be then? It's very strange. [*Goes away.*]

ANDREY: . . . Natasha is a good, honest woman, I tell you. When I married her, I thought we were going to be happy, I thought we should all be happy. – But – oh, my God! – [*Weeps.*] My dear sisters, my dear, good sisters, don't believe what I've been saying, don't believe it.

He goes, but only to be replaced by the ever-seeking Koolyghin, who calls through the door again with increased agitation: 'Where's Masha? Isn't Masha here? Extraordinary!' [*Goes away.*]

The bells of the horse-drawn fire-engine are heard again. They act as the death bell to all Masha's hopes:

IRENA: . . . Have you heard? The troops are being moved from the district – they're being sent somewhere a long way off . . . We'll be left quite alone then.

OLGA: Well?

IRENA: Olia, darling, I do respect the Baron – I think a lot of him, he's a very good man – I'll marry him . . . if only we can go to Moscow! Let's go, please do let's go! There's nowhere in all the world like Moscow . . .

The room is abandoned to the two sisters' restless slumber and to the leaping of the flames on the wall.

But fate was to take a hand in the docile Irena's decision to marry the Baron, and Chekhov threw the shadow of death's reaping scythe across a scarcely noticed scene in Act I where the sour Soliony is bickering with Toozenbach:

TOOZENBACH: . . . In twenty-five or thirty years' time every man and woman will be working. Every one of us!

CHEBUTYKIN: [*the sisters' uncle and a fast-failing army doctor*] I'm not going to work.

TOOZENBACH: You don't count.

SOLIONY: In twenty-five years' time you won't be alive, thank goodness. In a couple of years you'll die from a stroke – or I'll lose my temper with you and put a bullet in your head, my good fellow.

But in the event he shoots the Baron in an off-stage duel in the saddest act in all Chekhov.

In Act IV Chekhov takes us to the Prozorovs' old garden, which adjoins a plantation. Before the action proper begins we hear the voices of Rodé and some fellow officers calling their farewells to the trees. Their echoing voices add to the melancholy of the scene. We who have smiled and suffered with the sisters know that soon the brigade will be on the march to the brave, tear-compelling music of a military band.

Uncle Chebutykin, radiating the half-mischievous benevolence of an old man, sits ruminating. Koolyghin, sporting a decoration round his neck, is hovering, waiting, no doubt, for his wife. Irena and Toozenbach are bidding goodbye to two high-spirited junior officers, Rodé and Fedotik:

TOOZENBACH: . . . We've been good friends . . . Good-bye, my dear friends!

IRENA: Au revoir!

FEDOTIK: It's not 'au revoir'. It's good-bye. We shall never meet again!

KOOLYGHIN: Who knows? [*Wipes his eyes, smiling.*] There! you've made me cry.

IRENA: We'll meet some time.

FEDOTIK: Perhaps in ten or fifteen years' time. But then . . . We shall just meet and say: 'How are you?' coldly – [*he springs into action with his three-legged camera and takes a quick photograph*] Wait a moment – Just one more, for the last time.

RODE: [*Kisses Irena's hand.*] We're not likely to meet again – Thank you for everything – everything . . . [*looking up at the trees*] Good-bye trees! [*Shouts.*] Heigh-ho! Good-bye, echo!

It is from Andrey that we first receive news of the duel:

ANDREY: The town will seem quite empty. Life will be snuffed out like a candle. [*A pause.*] Something happened yesterday outside the theatre; everybody's talking about it. I'm the only one that doesn't seem to know about it.

CHEBUTYKIN: It was nothing. A lot of nonsense. Soliony started badgering the Baron, or something. The Baron lost his temper and insulted him, and in the end Soliony had to challenge him to a duel. [*Looks at his watch.*] I think it's time to go – At half-past twelve, in the forest over there, on the other side of the river . . . this is his [Soliony's] third duel.

Masha has been given over to sorrow:

MASHA: When you have to take your happiness in snatches . . . as I do, and then lose it, as I've lost it, you gradually get hardened and bad-tempered. [*Points at her breast.*] Something's boiling over inside me, here . . . All our hopes are gone. It's the same as when thousands of people haul a huge bell up into a tower. Untold labour and money is spent on it, and then suddenly it falls and gets smashed. Suddenly, without rhyme or reason.

Masha might unknowingly have been foretelling the Baron's knell. It is Chekhov's way of preparing the audience to accept the Baron's death. When Chebutykin speaks of Soliony's third duel Masha snaps back from her own sorrow:

MASHA: Whose third duel?
CHEBUTYKIN: Soliony's.

MASHA: [*alarmed*] What about the Baron?

CHEBUTYKIN: Well, what about him?

MASHA: My thoughts are all in a muddle – But what I mean to say is that they shouldn't be allowed to fight. He might wound the Baron or even kill him.

CHEBUTYKIN: The Baron's a good enough fellow, but what does it really matter if there's one Baron more or less in the world? . . .

ANDREY: I think it's simply immoral to fight a duel . . .

CHEBUTYKIN: That's only how it seems – We don't exist, nothing exists, it only seems to us that we do – And what difference does it make?

MASHA: [and with some justification, one must admit] Talk, talk, nothing but talk all day long! Having to live in this awful climate with the snow threatening to fall at any moment, and then on the top of it having to listen to all this sort of talk . . . Will you let me know when Vershinin comes? [*Walks off along the avenue.*] Look, the birds are beginning to fly away already! Swans or geese – Dear birds, happy birds.

ANDREY: [*to Chebutykin*] Our house will seem quite deserted. The officers will go, you'll go, my sister will get married, and I'll be left alone in the house.

CHEBUTYKIN: What about your wife?

ANDREY: My wife is my wife . . . there's something about her which pulls her down to the level of an animal – a sort of mean, blind, thick-skinned animal . . . I love Natasha, it's true. But at times she appears to me so utterly vulgar . . .

Shortly after, Soliony appears to remind the old doctor that it is the moment for them to set out for the duel:

SOLIONY: He had not time to say 'Oh, oh!'
        Before that bear had struck him low . . .

I shan't indulge in anything much, I'll just scorch his wings a little, like a woodcock's . . .

And now comes the Baron's parting from Irena:

TOOZENBACH: My dear, I'll be back in a moment.

IRENA: [*who knows nothing about the duel, but is uneasy*] Where are you going?

TOOZENBACH: . . . I want to see some of my colleagues off.

IRENA: . . . Nikolai, why are you so absent-minded today? What happened outside the theatre last night?

TOOZENBACH: [*with a movement of impatience*] I'll be back in an hour. [*Kisses her hands.*] . . . It's five years since I first began to love you, and still I can't get used to it, and you seem more beautiful every day. What wonderful, lovely hair! What marvellous eyes! I'll take you away tomorrow . . . And you'll be happy! But – there's only one 'but' . . . you don't love me!

IRENA: I can't help that! I'll be your wife, I'll be loyal and obedient . . . [*Weeps.*] I've never loved anyone in my life. Oh, I've had such dreams about being in love! I've been dreaming about it for ever so long, day and night – but somehow my soul seems like an expensive piano which someone has locked and the key's got lost.

TOOZENBACH: Such trifles, such silly little things sometimes become so important suddenly, for no apparent reason . . . you still regard them as trifles, and yet you suddenly find they're in control . . . Look at that dead tree, it's all dried-up, but it's still swaying in the wind along with the others. And in the same way, it seems to me that, if I die, I shall still have a share in life somehow . . .

IRENA: I'm coming with you.

TOOZENBACH: [*alarmed*] No, no! [*Goes off quickly, then stops in the avenue.*] Irena!

IRENA: What?

TOOZENBACH: [*striving to speak casually*] I didn't have any coffee this morning. Will you tell them to get some ready for me? [*Goes off quickly.*]

Vershinin calls to bid farewell to Masha, who has wandered away. 'What shall I philosophize about now?' he asks Olga, while he waits for Masha's return. He turns to Chekhov's original admirable and prophetic war-horse:

VERSHININ: In the old days the human race was always making war, its entire existence was taken up with campaigns, advances, retreats, victories – But now all that's out of date, and in its place there's a huge vacuum, clamouring to be filled. Humanity is passionately seeking something to fill it with and, of course, it will find something some day . . . If only we could educate the industrious people and make the educated people industrious! . . .

And now fate overtakes the sisters. Masha is torn from Vershinin's farewell embrace by Olga. Off-stage the regimental brass band plays a heart-breaking military march.

MASHA: The soldiers are going. Well – Happy journey to them! [*To her husband.*] We must go home . . .

But before the schoolmaster can collect her hat and coat, Doctor Chebutykin appears:

CHEBUTYKIN: Olga Serghyeevna! . . . [*Whispers into her ear.*]

OLGA: [*frightened*] It can't be true!

CHEBUTYKIN: Yes – a bad business – I'm so tired . . . I don't want to say another word – Anyway, nothing matters!

MASHA: What has happened?

OLGA: [*puts her arm round* IRENA] What a dreadful day! – I don't know how to tell you, dear.

IRENA: What is it? Tell me quickly, what is it? For Heaven's sake! – [*Cries.*]

CHEBUTYKIN: The Baron's just been killed in a duel.

IRENA: [*cries quietly*]. I knew it. I knew it.

CHEBUTYKIN: . . . [*Takes a newspaper out of his pocket.*] Let them cry for a bit. [*Sings quietly to himself.*] Tarara-boom-di-ay, I'm sitting on a tomb-di-ay . . .

[*The three sisters stand huddled together.*]

MASHA: [*through her grief*] Oh, listen to that band! They're leaving us – one of them's gone for good – for ever! We're left alone – to start our lives all over again. We must go on living – we must go on living.

Irena lays her head on Masha's breast and Chekhov is away on his vision – the vision he was born to voice:

IRENA: Some day people will know why such things happen, and what the purpose of all this suffering is . . . Meanwhile we must go on living – and working . . . It's autumn now, winter will soon be here, and the snow will cover everything – but I'll go on working and working!

OLGA: How cheerfully and jauntily that band's playing . . . Merciful God! The years will pass, and we shall all be gone for good and quite forgotten – Our faces and our voices will be forgotten and people won't even know that there were once three of us here – But our sufferings may mean happiness for the people who come after us – There'll be a time when peace and happiness reign in the world, and then we shall be remembered kindly and blessed. No, my dear sisters, life isn't finished for us yet . . . The band is playing so cheerfully and joyfully – maybe, if we wait a little longer, we shall find out why we live, why we suffer . . . Oh, if we only knew, if only we knew!

CURTAIN

Laurence Olivier's production of *The Three Sisters* for the National Theatre provided the twenty-first-and-a-half sister that I have seen, take a sibling, give a sibling. The half was supplied by the Actors' Studio of New York, who were appearing in London, the glories of which I forfeited at the first interval, and did not shed one longing, lingering look behind. Television supplied the twenty-fourth-and-a-half sister soon afterwards.

Naturally, with so many sisters remembered, half-remembered and read about, the Sister syndrome is apt to merge. Did I, for instance, see with my own eyes the leaping flames of a provincial town on fire, bringing the walls of the sisters' bedroom to life in the reflected glow of the Kommisarjevsky production? Or did I only read about the quiet shadows of two of that eloquent and mournful trio, combing their hair behind the screens that modestly kept secret their night attire? No, I must have seen it, even though I hardly knew what it was I was seeing; far less, at that time, could I measure it against my own, my ordered London life, for was not serene and lovely Margaret Swallow, the Masha, sitting reading in the green shadow of an off-stage tree? Poor lady, she should have lived hereafter. There would have been a time – and a greater need – for such serenity. Not that there could ever be a time or word that could describe the utter desolation with which the untimely death of a young actress strikes the heart.

By 1935, the year of Harcourt Williams's production of the play for the Old Vic, I was far more aware and receptive. Going back to the Prozorovs again and yet again, I came to know them rather better than my own kin: the Masha so eloquently played by Vivienne Bennett; Olga, the practical, with the throbbing temples of the middle-aged spinster, living in the still of Marie Ney's mind, and beautifully communicated to us; and an un-remembered, but no doubt suitable Irena, Nancy Hornby. Cecil

Trouncer, a golden actor in the autumn of his days, played the old Doctor Chebutykin, a figure for affection, with nothing of the old lecher who lurks under the amiable surface.

Gielgud was the Vershinin in Michel Saint-Denis's production in 1938, part-Russian intellectual, part-brother Val, with that cool St Elmo's fire which is Sir John's own magical gift, opposite Peggy Ashcroft's child-like Irena, grave and gay and then in April fashion: both matched by Michael Redgrave's sunny, boater-hatted Baron Toozenbach, standing before her stammering between hope and fate, in their last scene together. Nor could I forget Frederick Lloyd's comfortably creased and believable old reprobate Chebutykin, and the no-nonsense Natasha of Angela Baddeley wed to George Devine's Andrey, who wore his carpet slippers in his hen-pecked soul. Can this cast ever have been bettered? Not, I would say, in its British way.

The British, however, are apt to play their Chekhov with their gloves on – they might almost be dancing *Les Sylphides* – insulated in the kind of holy hush that Chekhov himself would have hated for his sturdy characters. Chekhov who saw his fellow-Russians clearly: laughter, tears, love, frustration, gaiety and guilt, all bubbling in the samovar. 'Perhaps,' Chekhov wrote to Vishnevsky, 'what I am turning out is not a play, but wearisome Crimean fiddle-faddle. . . . *The Three Sisters* is very difficult to write, more difficult than my other plays.'

Sturdy is the easy definition of Olivier's *Three Sisters* for the National Theatre, with Joan Plowright sturdiest of all – a down-to-earth Masha – if the good earth were all. But then, perhaps the three daughters of a Russian general are of the earth earthier than a Sandhurst sisterhood might turn out to be.

Marianne Faithfull, working on the other side of the scale from Joan Plowright, in an earlier Royal Court Theatre production, took a bland and milky way. Her Irena was a docile and translucent girl, like candlelight shining behind an alabaster screen. In this production Glenda Jackson's 'mod' Masha tore apart the famous non-road to Moscow, stone from stone and cobble from cobble.

Six of my three sisters travelled to London from afar, with the Moscow Art Theatre and the Theatre Beyond the Gate from Czechoslovakia, laughing, weeping, and living, in both productions, in the inner motif of an embroidery of sound. Indeed sound seemed to motivate Krejca's unforgettable production. Pace quickens and lessens with the dance music and the sounds of distant guitars, the wind in the telegraph wires outside, the tolling of church bells and the trundling of the horse-drawn fire-engines; the tender echo of the farewell called out to the trees by the departing soldiers, and the brave music of their passing band.

Looking along my line of sighing sisters, the Masha who most makes her love and tears my own is Marie Tomasova in this Czech production. The moment in it that remains with me is that of three distracted ladies circling the stage, wounded creatures that they are, in their despair, as the garrison goes.

What light has television thrown on the dreaming girls with Moscow on their minds? The close-up and the cut and cross-cut, which are the conversation of the camera, isolate and underline their longing and the claustrophobia of their provincial exile. We may be sure that for the sisters, in the words of the Russian proverb, 'it would have been better to travel hopefully than to arrive'. What then, did we look for from Eileen Atkins, Janet Suzman and Michelle Dotrice? A green thought in a green shade, of a small world on a small screen?

Amorphous, yes. Yet in some magical Chekhovian way the plot line seems to spin itself out of the characterization, so that plot and people grow out of the nebulous atmosphere together; and if to write a play in this way is not one of stagecraft's great mysteries, great miracles, I know of none other.

The Cherry Orchard

Only six months after he had completed *The Three Sisters* Chekhov was already simmering *The Cherry Orchard*. On 7 March 1901 he told his wife that his next play was to be 'amusing – at least in conception', and amusing *The Cherry Orchard* is, as well as nostalgic, heart-breaking and prophetic, for in it the white blossom, like the old order, passeth: 'The sun has set, my friends,' says Gaev and we, with hindsight, know that in these six words he is sounding the knell of a way of life – a leisured and elegant way of life, that was nearing its close. After Gaev, the deluge.

In January 1902 *The Cherry Orchard* was still fallowing – still in that no-brains-land where an author hesitates to disturb it lest the dimly outlined branches bear no bloom: 'I am only able to catch a faint glimmer of it, like the faint glimmer of an early dawn,' he wrote, 'and I myself do not understand what it is really like or what form it is likely to assume, for it changes every day.' Like spring? But in Chekhov's case the germination was to prove a long process. He had the vision, the Genesis, but lacked the strength to write the play:

Yalta, January 27, 1903

Dear Vera Fyodorovna [Vera Kommisarjevskaya],
Many thanks for your letter. Not many thanks, multitudinous thanks ... Let me tell you the following about the play:
(1) It's true I've got an idea for a play and a title for it (*The Cherry Orchard*, but that's still a secret), and I'll most likely settle down to writing no later than the end of February, provided of course I'm well; (2) the central role in the play is that of an old woman, to the author's great regret; and (3) ... why don't I write a play for *you*. Not for this or that theatre, but simply for you. It's an old dream of mine. Well, it's all in God's hands. If my health were what it used to be, I wouldn't waste time talking; I'd sit right down and start writing the play on the spot. I've had pleurisy since December – can you imagine? – and I'm leaving the house tomorrow for the first time since being confined for so long. ...

You write, 'I am proceeding on the strength of my faith which, if it breaks, will kill within me ...' That's entirely as it should be. You're quite right, but for heaven's sake, don't stake it all on the new theatre. After all, you're an actress, and being an actress is like being a good sailor: no matter what ship he sails, be it government- or private-owned, in all places, under all conditions he always remains a good sailor.

And so a date for beginning *The Cherry Orchard* seemed settled. To Olga Knipper he wrote:

Yalta, February 11, 1903

My incomparable wife.
... The almond buds have already turned white, the garden will soon be in blossom ...

I shall start work on the play on February 21. You will have the part of a foolish girl ...

At first Chekhov meant Olga Knipper to play the part of Varia, but in the event she played Madame Ranyevskaia. But in the matter of a February start Chekhov's '21st' was over-optimistic. In another letter to Olga Knipper he wrote:

Yalta, March 4, 1903

... As for the play, you have apparently forgotten that since the time of Noah I have been telling each and every one that I will work on it late in February or early in March. My laziness has nothing to do with the matter. I am not my own enemy, you know, and if I had the strength I would write not one but twenty-five plays ...

By 5-6 March 1903 it is clear that a start has been made:

Yalta, March 5-6, 1903

My darling actressella, as I am no longer a man of letters but a gourmet, today I went to Kuba's shop ... They have marvellous caviar, enormous olives, sausage made on the premises and which must be fried at home (very delicious!), cured fillet of sturgeon, ham, biscuits, mushrooms. ... In short, there is no longer any need to bring anything from Moscow, except groats and millet ... Altschuller was here today and insisted that under no circumstances should I go to Moscow before the middle of April. My darling, my wife, my actress, my own, won't you find it possible to come to Yalta during the Easter week, or if the company goes to Petersburg, on the feast of St Thomas the following week? We would have a glorious time together. I would give you delicious things to drink and to eat, and *The Cherry Orchard* to read ...

In *The Cherry Orchard* you will be ... Varia, the adopted daughter, twenty-two years old ...

There is a high wind today . . . If my play doesn't come out as I conceived it, you may punch my head. Stanislavski's part is comic, and so is yours.

News of the play, which understandably enough was not yet finished, was sent to Stanislavski at the end of July:

July 28, 1903, Yalta

Dear Konstantin Sergeyevich,
. . . My play [*The Cherry Orchard*] is not done and is moving ahead a little stiffly, a state of affairs I attribute to my laziness, the marvellous weather and the difficulty of the subject. I will write you when I finish, or better yet will wire. Your rôle [Lopahin], it seems, has come off not badly, though I won't set myself up as a judge, because generally speaking I can hardly form an estimate of a play merely by reading it . . .
Yours,

A. Chekhov

I won't read my play to you because I don't know how to; but I'll give it to you for reading, providing I can get it ready, of course.

But in the middle of September Chekhov's last play was still being hampered by his health, as we see in a letter he wrote to M. P. Lilina:

Yalta, September 15, 1903

Dear Mariya Petrovna,
Don't believe anybody, not a single living soul has read my play; for you I have written the part not of a 'bigot,' but of a very lovely girl, a role with which, I hope, you will be satisfied . . . Olga will not take the play with her, I'll send her all four acts as soon as I can do a whole day's work. It has turned out not a drama but a comedy, in places even a farce, and I am afraid that I'll catch it from Vladimir Ivanovich

[Nemirovich-Danchenko]. Konstantin Sergeyevich has a big role. Generally speaking, there are not many roles.

I cannot come for the opening; I'll stay in Yalta till November . . . As a writer, it is essential for me to observe as many women as possible, to study them and consequently, I regret to say, I cannot be a faithful husband. Inasmuch as I observe women chiefly for plays, it is my opinion that the Art Theatre should raise my wife's salary or grant her a pension . . .

When you see Vishnevsky, tell him that he should try to reduce [his weight] – this is necessary for my play. . . .

Chekhov, we now know, had privately cast Vishnevsky for the role of Gaev, most lovable of incompetents.

A fortnight later we see Gaev through the eyes of Chekhov, in a letter to Olga Knipper:

Yalta, September 23, 1903

Greetings, my sweet, my better little half! . . .

The fourth act of my play, as compared with the other acts, will be skimpy as to content yet effective. The way your part ends does not seem bad to me. In any event don't be downhearted; everything is going well . . .

Regards to Vishnevsky and tell him to start soaking up suavity and refinement for a role in my play . . .

One more week and the first draft of the play is finished:

Yalta, September 27, 1903

My darling, my pony, I have already telegraphed you that the play is finished . . . I am already making a copy. My people have turned out to be alive, true enough [dear Chekhov, what a relief that must have been to him!], but what the play itself is like I don't know. There, I shall send you the play; you will read it and find out . . .

... I am writing *The Cherry Orchard* on that same paper which Nemirovich gave me and with the gold pens which I also received from him. Whether this will make for any changes is something I do not know ...

By 9 October he was more confident about the play. He wrote to Olga Knipper from Yalta:

... My mood is excellent. I am copying the play, shall soon finish, my dear, I swear ... I assure you every extra day is only to the good, for my play becomes better and better, and the characters are clear now. Only I am afraid there are passages that the censor will strike out, which will be dreadful.

My own, my dove, darling, pony, don't be uneasy, everything is not as bad as you think, everything is going very well. I swear that the play is ready. I assure you a thousand times. If I didn't send it to you earlier, it is only because I have been copying it too slowly and making changes, as I always do when I copy ...

Darling, I will certainly come to Moscow even if you kill me, and I would have come even if I weren't married; consequently, if I am run over by a cab in Moscow, you won't be guilty.

Act well, carefully; study, darling, observe; you are still a young actress ...

... The Lord be with you, be at peace and cheerful.

Your A.

But on 19 October, while Chekhov was awaiting the verdict on his play, self-doubt came back, as the following letter to his wife shows:

Greetings, sweet horsy, my darling,
I didn't write you yesterday because I was waiting with trepidation for a telegram all day. Late last night your

telegram came, and early this morning I got a hundred-eighty-word telegram from Vladimir Ivanovich [Nemirovich-Danchenko]. ... I was so worried, so afraid. The things that worried me most of all were the second act's lack of movement and a certain sketchy quality in the role of Trofimov, the student. After all, Trofimov is constantly being sent into exile, he is constantly being expelled from the university. How can you put all those things across?

... If somebody's coming this way, don't bother about sending my cap; send me a package of ... stationery (the cheapest) and some other exciting things ...

Is my play going to be performed? If so, when? [The poor, patient playwright's perpetual question comes echoing down to us through the years.] The Odessa newspapers have reported the plot of my play. It doesn't resemble it at all.

The next note to Olga Knipper shows Chekhov's humility – where a second-ranking writer might make a stand and refuse to rewrite, Chekhov is willing to recast an entire act:

October 23, 1903, Yalta
You write that Vishnevsky can't play Gaev. Well, who then? Stanislavski? Then who'll play Lopakhin? ...

Nemirovich writes that my play has a lot of tears and a certain amount of coarseness. Write and tell me what you think is wrong, darling, and what they say, and I'll correct it. It's not too late, you know; I could still rework an entire act.

This letter includes an account of a guest that, with its inconsequence, might have come straight out of one of Chekhov's plays: 'That tall Olga Mikhailovna came to see us yesterday. She discussed love and promised to send some herring.'

Directors could do worse than benefit by Chekhov's clarification of mood rather than tears indicating his intention when he writes the instruction: *through her tears*, in his stage directions. He enlarges upon his intention in the following letter to Nemirovich-Danchenko:

> *October 23, 1903, Yalta*
>
> ... I'm afraid Anya will speak in a tearful tone of voice (for some reason you find her similar to Irena), I'm afraid she won't be played by a young actress. Anya never once cries in the play and nowhere does she even have tears in her voice. She may have tears in her eyes during the second act, but her tone of voice is gay and lively. Why do you say in your telegram that there are many weepy people in my play? Where are they? Varia's the only one, and that's because she's a crybaby by nature. Her tears are not meant to make the spectator feel despondent. I often use 'through her tears' in my stage directions, but that indicates only a character's mood, not actual tears. There's no cemetery in the second act.
>
> ... I haven't seen *Lower Depths* or *Julius Caesar*. If I could go to Moscow now, I'd be in a state of bliss for a whole week ...

Chekhov's description of Lopakhin in his letter to Stanislavski: has a curiously British ring about it – 'a very decent chap':

> *Yalta,*
> *October 30, 1903*
>
> ... As I worked on Lopakhin I thought of him as your role. If for any reason he doesn't appeal to you, take Gaev. Lopakhin may be a merchant, but he is a decent person in every sense; his behaviour must be entirely proper, cultivated and free of pettiness or clowning. I had the feeling you could do a brilliant job of this role, the central role in the play ... Leonidov would turn it into a cute little Kulak. When you're selecting an actor for the role, don't forget that Varia, a serious and religious young lady, is in love with Lopakhin; she could never have loved a cute little Kulak.

Long-distance casting is always the devil for a dramatist:

Yalta,
November 2, 1903

Dear Vladimir Ivanovich [Nemirovich-Danchenko],
Two letters from you in one day! ...

1. Anya can be played by anyone at all, even a complete unknown, as long as she is young and looks like a little girl and speaks in a youthful, vibrant voice. It's not a particularly important role. [Despite Chekhov's emphasis on a young Anya, the part was, finally, given to Maria Liliuc, who was thirty-seven at the time. Lopakhin was played by Leonidov, the actor Chekhov thought the least suited to the part.]

2. Varia is a much more important role. What about having Maria Petrovna play her? Without Maria Petrovna the role will seem flat and crude, and I'll have to rework it, tone it down. Maria Petrovna doesn't have to worry about being typecast, because in the first place she is a talented person, and in the second, Varia isn't at all like Sonia or Natasha; she wears black, she's a nun, she's slightly simple-minded, a crybaby, and so on ...

3. Gaev and Lopakhin are roles for Konstantin Sergeyevich to try out and choose from. If he were to take Lopakhin and do well in the role the play would be a success. Because if Lopakhin is ... portrayed by a pallid actor, then both the role and the play are ruined.

4. Pishchik is for Gribunin. For heaven's sake, don't give the role to Vishnevsky.

5. Charlotte is an important role. You can't give it to Pomyalova, of course. Muratova might be good, but she's not funny. This is Miss Knipper's role.

6. Yepikhodov – if Moskvin wants it, so be it ... [Moskvin did, and played it for decades to come.]

7. Firs is for Artyom. [Lucky Artyom! I have never seen an altogether bad Firs.]

8. Dunyasha is for Khalyutina.

9. Yasha. If the Alexandrov you wrote me about is . . . your assistant director, then let him have Yasha. Moskvin would make a wonderful Yasha. Nor do I have anything against Leonidov.

10. The Passerby is for Gromov.

11. The Stationmaster who recites 'The Peccatrix' in the third act is for an actor with a bass voice.

Charlotte speaks correct, not broken Russian, but every once in a while she hardens a final soft consonant . . . [Clearly Chekhov was anxious lest Kommissarhevsky should make Charlotte be played with a broad and comic German accent.] Pishchik is a true Russian, an old man afflicted by the gout, old age and too much to eat; he is stout and wears a long coat . . . and boots without heels. Lopakhin wears a white vest and yellow shoes; he takes big steps and waves his arms as he walks. He thinks while he walks and walks in a straight line. Since his hair is rather long, he often tosses his head back. When lost in thought, he strokes his beard from back to front, that is, from neck to mouth. Trofimov is clear, I think. [Chekhov nicknamed him 'two-and-twenty misfortunes' thus putting the nature of the clerk beyond doubt.] Varia wears a black dress with a wide belt.

For three years I've been planning to write *The Cherry Orchard*, and for three years I've been telling you to engage an actress to play the role of Lyubov Andreyevna [This figures still in the working life of a dramatist.] And now you're stuck with a game of solitaire that is not working out.

Chekhov had intended the role of Ranyevskaia to be played by an elderly actress (we come upon Liubov in the throes of a last love). But in the end it went to Olga Knipper, who subsequently played it well into the 1930s. Because of this circumstance it has become more or less traditional to cast it with a much younger actress than Chekhov wrote about. The managerial practice of wishing always to cast from players already in the company can be a sore trial to the dramatist. He concludes his letter to Nemirovich-Danchenko:

> Why is Maria Petrovna so determined to play Anya? And why does Maria Fyodorovna think she's too aristocratic for Varia? . . . Oh, let them do what thcy want.

Earlier in the letter he writes:

> I'm in the most idiotic situation imaginable: I'm trapped here all alone with no idea why. And you are wrong to say that, despite all your work, it is 'Stanislavski's theatre.' It is only you they talk about, only you they write about, while Stanislavski is being criticized for his Brutus. If you leave, I leave. Gorky is younger than we are . . . As for the theatre in Nizhny Novgorod, that's a passing fancy; Gorky will give it a try, have a taste of it and drop it. By the way, both theatres for the people and literature for the people are ridiculous; they're all merely lollipops for the people. What needs to be done is not lower Gogol down to the people's level, but raise the people to Gogol's level.

To educate the people – this was the perennial aim of Chekhov – the doctor-turned-playwright.

Yalta, November 23, 1903
Dear Konstantin Sergeyevich [K. S. Stanislavski],
Hay-making takes place June 20-25, by that time the corn-crake's rasping cry is no longer heard, the frogs are also silent by then. The oriole alone moans plaintively. There is no cemetery, there was one, but a very long time ago. Two or

three gravestones lying helter-skelter are all that remains. A bridge – that's very good. If a train can be shown without noise, without a single sound – go to it. I am not against the same scenery in Acts III and IV, except that it would be convenient to have exits and entrances in Act IV.

I am impatiently waiting for the day and the hour when my wife will at last permit me to come to Moscow . . . [Two days earlier he had written to Olga: 'I keep waiting for you to allow me to pack and start for Moscow.' 'To Moscow, to Moscow!' This is the cry not of *Three Sisters* but of *One Husband*.]

I sit in my study and keep glancing at the telephone. Telegrams are read to me over it, and so I wait for the moment when I shall finally be summoned to Moscow.

Eight days later he again wrote to Olga Knipper:

Yalta, November 29, 1903

. . . They persist in failing to summon me to Moscow, and apparently don't want to know me. You ought to write me frankly why this is so, what the reason is . . . If you knew how drearily the rain hammers on the roof, how much I want to have a look at my wife . . .

Schnapp, I repeat, is not the right sort. What is needed is a doleful fool or something of the kind. You can do without a dog.

Well, I hug you.

Chekhov is referring to the dog he needed to appear in Act I of *The Cherry Orchard*. The dog has become legendary in the theatre by reason of the speech with which it is introduced:

CHARLOTTA: My dog eats nuts, too.

The accent can fall on any of its monosyllables and will always make sense, and no Charlotta has settled the stress definitely.

In the first week in December Chekhov's doctor allowed him

to go to Moscow so that he could be present at some rehearsals of *The Cherry Orchard*. He criticized the acting, made changes in the text and wrote new passages for those the censor had cut.

The cast was bewildered and lackadaisical and Chekhov wrote to ask his friend, F. D. Batyushkov, to postpone his visit to the new play. Soon the cast was to settle down.

Moscow, January 19, 1904

... On January 17, [1904] when *The Cherry Orchard* opened, my twenty-fifth anniversary [the twenty-fifth anniversary of his first publication – there was some uncertainty about the year] was celebrated on such a large scale, so warmly and indeed, so unexpectedly, that I have not yet been able to regain my composure.

[It was arranged, writes Yarmolinsky in a footnote, that the play should open on Chekhov's birthday, though there was some argument about when that might be. Nervous that the play might be a failure, he was not present for the first two acts, but ... appeared during the interval before Act IV. There was a tremendous ovation and thirteen speeches, the last being delivered by Chaliapin at the supper which was given after the performance.]

It would be well if you came by Shrovetide. I think that only by then will our actors have come to themselves and play *The Cherry Orchard* not with such bewilderment and so lackadaisically as they do now.

So often we find Chekhov protesting that his plays are not high dramas but comedies of manners:

Yalta, April 10, 1904

My sweet little linnet [Olga Knipper],
... Why on posters and in newspaper advertisements is my play stubbornly called a drama? Nemirovich and Alekseyev

positively do not see in my play what I wrote, and I am ready to vouch that neither of them read *The Cherry Orchard* through carefully even once . . . I assure you. I have in mind not alone the dreadful stage set of the second act, not alone Khalyutina, replaced by Adurskaya, who does the same thing and decidedly nothing of what is in my text.

The weather is warm, but it is chilly in the shade; the evenings are cold. I take walks lazily, because for some reason I gasp for breath. [But none more than Chekhov, a doctor, knew better what that 'some reason' was.] *The Cherry Orchard* is being given here by touring trash. [The 'touring trash' turned out to be the Sevastopol Municipal Theatre Company.]

. . . Do not forget me, think sometimes about the man to whom you were married once upon a time . . .

Your poor stick.

In his next letter to Olga Knipper he wrote of provincial players, together with some affectionate domesticities – so much a part of Chekhov, the husband who married late and was already an invalid:

Yalta, April 15, 1904

My sweet, good darling, yesterday there was no letter from you, today again no letter; in this Yalta I am as alone as a comet, and I am not particularly well. The day before yesterday in the local theatre (without wings or dressing rooms) *The Cherry Orchard* was staged, the *mise-en-scène* being that of the Art Theatre, the actors a vile lot headed by Daryalova (so named, aping the actress, Daryal), and there are notices, and tomorrow there will be notices and the day after tomorrow too. I am called to the telephone, acquaintances sigh, and I, a patient, so to speak, who is being treated here must dream of how to make off . . . I must confess that provincial actors behave just like scoundrels.

... I can't stay here: upset stomach, actors, the public, telephone calls, and the devil knows what.

What are your takings these days? Really full houses? I can imagine how tired out you all are. Meanwhile I sit still and keep dreaming about fishing ... although in the entire summer I shall land only one gudgeon, and he will be caught due to his suicidal disposition.

... I love you, you know, I love your letters, your acting, your manner of walking. The only thing I don't like is when you dawdle over the washstand.

Your A.

A touch of the blarney to the rescue?

Moscow,
January 6, 1904

Dear Vera Fyodorovna [Vera Kommisarjevskaya],

Where are you? In Baku, Tiflis, Harkov? ...

I haven't seen Savina nor been in correspondence with her, and it never occurred to me to give *Cherry Orchard* to the Empress Alexandra Theatre. The play belongs to the Art Theatre ... for both Moscow and Petersburg ...

The reason I can tell you this so light-heartedly is that I am firmly convinced that my *Cherry Orchard* is not at all suitable for you. The central female role in the play is an old woman who lives entirely in the past and has nothing in the present ... the other female part, are more or less minor and lacking in subtlety, and are of no interest to you. My play will soon be published ... and if you read it you'll see for yourself that there is nothing in it to interest you, no matter how indulgent you feel toward it.

... I wish you health, strength, success, and – at least one day a week – complete and utter happiness ...

Chekhov was surprised and relieved when his *Cherry Orchard* was a success wherever it was given:

> *Yalta,*
> *February 27, 1904*

My fine spouse,

... *The Cherry Orchard* is having three or four performances in every city; it's a success, can you imagine? I've just been reading about Rostov-on-the-Don, where it is having its third performance ...

Well, God be with you, darling, my kind, affable little puppy ...

By the time that Chekhov was writing *The Cherry Orchard*, Nemirovich-Danchenko writes in his memoirs *Out of the Past*, the literate public were aware that his days were numbered and every new work was received with tender gratitude, with the realization that it was written with what was left of his dwindling strength. Yet the play suffered in no way from its writer's increasing weakness.

The Cherry Orchard is sharp comedy. Nowhere else does Chekhov say so clearly that the world these people made for themselves, would have to end in a whimper.

A white waistcoat and brown shoes; a cherry orchard. And somewhere in between the two concepts hovers Chekhov's play of dispossession, which the dramatist always maintained was a comedy, and Stanislavski, the *entrepreneur*, hailed as a tragedy. One is reminded of the old French definition: 'Life is a comedy to him who thinks, a tragedy to him who feels.' Chekhov's strength is that he both felt and thought.

The white waistcoat and brown shoes worn (at Chekhov's insistence) by Lopakhin, ex-peasant and man of business, represent the new order; and the cherry orchard – those avenues of A. E. Housman's 'loveliest of trees', floating their sea of white blossoms – symbolizes the old order which, it is conceded generally, passeth. Lopakhin, whose father, like Chekhov's father, kept a mean, dark little shop in the village, is the stone flung by fate to punctuate the fecklessness of the family Gaev. We come upon him waiting for the return of Madame Ranyevskaia and her entourage in their old home cradled by the gently waving branches. We are given a fully stated characterization of Lopakhin at the opening of the play, in his third speech:

LOPAKHIN ... Liubov Andryeevna [Madame Ranyevskaia] has been abroad for five years, I don't know what she's like now. – She used to be a good soul. An easy-going, simple kind of person. I remember when I was a boy of about fifteen, my father – he had a small shop in the village then – hit me in the face and made my nose bleed [so, indeed, had Chekhov's father, a religious man, treated him: 'I never could forgive my father for having whipped me when I was quite small,' Chekhov recorded]. – We had come to the manor for something or other, and he'd been drinking ... Liubov Andryeevna – she was still young and slender – brought me in and took me to the washstand in this very room, the nursery it was then. 'Don't cry, little peasant,' she said, 'it'll be better before you're old enough to get married'. [*Pause.*] 'Little peasant' – She was right enough, my father was a peasant. [And it is not forgotten that Chekhov's paternal grandfather had bought himself and his family out of serfdom] Yet here I am – all dressed up in a white waistcoat and brown shoes. – But you can't make a silk purse out of a sow's ear. I am rich, I've got a lot of money, but anyone can see I'm just a peasant, anyone who takes the trouble to think about me and look under my skin. [*Turns over pages in the book.*] I've been reading this book, and

I haven't understood a word of it. I fell asleep reading it.

In this speech lies the core of the motivation that makes Lopakhin, almost in spite of himself, bid for and finally buy himself the cherry orchard, and the reason, too, why he lacks the courage to ask Madame Ranyevskaia's step-daughter Varia to marry him. 'Merciful God!' he says to Madame Ranyevskaia, 'My father was your father's serf, and your grandfather's too, but you did so much for me in the past that I forget everything and I love you as if you were my own sister – more than my own sister.

Here, for the first time in the play, we hear the knell of the cherry orchard. Lopakhin tolls the bell, as it were. This he will do at intervals throughout the play:

LOPAKHIN: ... You know, of course, that your cherry orchard is going to be sold to pay your debts. The auction is to take place on the twenty-second of August, but there's no need for you to worry. You can sleep in peace, my dear; there's a way out. This is my plan, please listen carefully. [Hope springs eternal . . .] Your estate is only twenty miles from town, and the railway line is not far away. Now, if your cherry orchard and the land along the river are divided into plots and leased out for summer residences you'll have a yearly income of at least twenty-five thousand roubles. . . . You'll charge the tenants at least twenty-five roubles a year for a plot of one acre, and if you advertise now, I'm prepared to stake any amount you like that you won't have a spot of land unoccupied by the autumn: it will be snatched up . . . I must congratulate you, you're saved after all . . . of course . . . all the old outbuildings will have to be pulled down, as well as this house which is no good to anybody. The old cherry orchard should be cut down, too.

To which Madame Ranyevskaia replies, as we might have expected:

> LIUBOV ANDRYEEVNA: Cut down? My dear man, forgive me, you don't seem to understand. If there's one thing interesting, one thing really outstanding in the whole county, it's our cherry orchard.

Lopakhin answers mutinously:

> LOPAKHIN: The only outstanding thing about this orchard is that it's very large. It only produces a crop every other year, and then there's nobody to buy it.
> GAEV: This orchard is actually mentioned in the Encyclopaedia.

And Lopakhin, the patient, if not tactful, Lopakhin, says:

> LOPAKHIN: If you can't think clearly about it, or come to a decision, the cherry orchard and the whole estate as well will be sold by auction . . . There's no other way.

Thus the first shots in a long siege have been exchanged in this comedy of dispossession which will be so feelingly told – it is as though Chekhov were watching some friendly neighbours over the garden wall, extending his laughing sympathy to them as they are evicted. Other people's misfortunes? Yes, but seen through the eyes of commiseration, for Chekhov, one of a sprawling, poverty-stricken family, had first-hand knowledge of the desperate woes of dispossession.

In many ways *The Cherry Orchard* reflects the drift of the land-owning classes towards catastrophe in the small years of the nineteenth century more completely than any other play within the Chekhovian canon. Heavy with blossom, it ignores the tide of events, making no leeway, making no attempt to change with the wind of change: 'It only produces a crop [of cherries] every other year,' says Lopakhin, 'and then there's nobody to buy it.' After its own fashion it reflects its owners' lassitude and foretells their fate, weighted as they are with anxiety, unable to challenge destiny. One finds it hard to contemplate the ultimate fate of the drifting, shiftless family Gaev and their cherry trees, aimlessly awaiting the revolution which already clouds the skies ahead, which they are powerless to avert and which will certainly overtake them.

Liubov Ranyevskaia is the other side of the coin from Arkadina in *The Seagull*: Arkadina, so selfish, mean and ungenerous, understanding no problem save her own; Ranyevskaia, prodigal and spendthrift, who would give away her last kopeck, so closely touched is she by the troubles of those around her.

Anya, Ranyevskaia's seventeen-year-old daughter, gives us an impressionist's glimpse of her mother in Paris and on a journey which highlights Liubov's nature in Act I:

ANYA: . . . In Paris it was cold and snowing . . . Mamma was living on the fifth floor, and when I got there she had visitors. There were some French ladies there and an old priest with a little book, and the room was full of cigarette smoke, so untidy and uncomfortable. Suddenly I felt so sorry for Mamma, so sorry, that I took her head between my hands, and just couldn't let it go. – Afterwards Mamma cried and was very sweet to me . . . She had already sold her villa near Mentone, she had nothing left, positively nothing. I hadn't any money left either . . . I had hardly enough to get to Paris. And Mamma couldn't grasp that! In station restaurants she would order the most expensive dishes and tip the waiters a rouble each . . .

And we are to find that Liubov Ranyevskaia is as extravagant with her sympathy as with her money:

> VARIA: Dear Mamma is just the same as she used to be, she hasn't changed a bit. If she had her own way, she'd give away everything.

Take her impulsive way of life as we see it in Act II, where we come upon the Gaevs and their entourage sitting among some ancient tombstones in what, a long time ago, must have been the village graveyard: 'Sister has not got out of the habit of flinging away her money,' observes Gaev, who himself has been accused of eating away his property in the form of the caramels he nibbles all the time – Gaev, the man of two passions, caramels and billiards. And here we come upon her doing it, giving at the same time from her purse and her generous heart:

> LIUBOV ANDRYEEVNA [RANYEVSKAIA]: [*looking in her purse*] Yesterday I had a lot of money but today there's hardly any left. My poor Varia is feeding everyone on milk soups to economize; the old servants in the kitchen get nothing but dried peas to eat and here I am spending money senselessly ... [*She drops the purse, scattering gold coins.*] Now I've scattered it all over the place ... Why did I go out to lunch? ... That restaurant of yours, with its beastly music; and the table-cloths smelt of soap ...

In this scene Lopakhin rails at them:

> LOPAKHIN: You must forgive me for saying it, but really I've never met such feckless, unbusiness-like, queer people as you are. You are told in plain language that your estate is up for sale, and you simply don't seem to understand it.
>
> LIUBOV ANDRYEEVNA: But what are we to do? Tell us, what?
>
> LOPAKHIN: I keep on telling you. Every day I tell you the same thing. You must lease the cherry orchard and the land

for villas, and you must do it now, as soon as possible. The auction is going to be held almost at once. Please do try to understand! Once you definitely decide to have the villas, you'll be able to borrow as much money as you like, and then you'll be out of the wood.

LIUBOV ANDRYEEVNA: [*distastefully*] Villas and summer visitors! Forgive me, but it's so vulgar.

LOPAKHIN: [*flings up his arms*] Honestly, I feel I shall burst into tears, or shriek, or fall down and faint. I simply can't stand it. You've literally worn me out . . .

It is in this scene that Chekhov has written of Ranyevskaia's past as seen through her own eyes, in a passage as full of the pain of her little history as anything, yet as matter of fact as any passage in Ibsen's plays not excluding *Little Eyolf*. Already, in Act I, Anya has told us of the drowning of Liubov's son:

ANYA: It was six years ago that Father died, and then only a month after that, little brother Grisha was drowned in the river. He was only seven, such a pretty little boy! Mamma couldn't bear it and went away – she never looked back. [*Shivers.*] How well I understand her! If she only knew . . .

Now in the one-time graveyard in Act II, Ranyevskaia relates her past sins to her present distress:

LIUBOV ANDRYEEVNA: Oh, my sins! Look at the way I've always squandered money, continually. It was sheer madness. And then I got married to a man who only knew how to get into debt. Champagne killed him – he was a terrific drinker – and then, worse luck, I fell in love with someone else – it was my first punishment, a blow straight to my heart – my little boy was drowned here, in this river – and then I went abroad. I went away for good, and never meant to return, I never meant to see the river again - I just shut my eyes and ran away in a frenzy of grief, but - *he* followed me. It was so cruel and brutal of him! I bought a villa near Mentone, because he fell ill there, you see, and for three years I never had any rest, day or night. He was a sick man, he quite wore me out; my soul seemed to dry right up. Then, last year when the villa had to be sold to pay the debts, I went to Paris, and there he robbed me and left me; he went away and lived with another woman. - I tried to poison myself - so foolish, so shameful! And then suddenly I felt an urge to come back to Russia, to my own country and my little girl. - [*Wipes away her tears.*] Oh, Lord, Lord, be merciful, forgive me my sins! Don't punish me any more . . .

Here we have the root of the matter. Ranyevskaia has come home in a confetti of wires from her lover in Paris. Come home to preside over the sale of her old home with its cherry orchard - she had, after all, brought herself to part with her villa in Mentone. But there is still one hope, one golden, tantalizing hope, urging her to hang on; and hope takes the off-stage form of an aunt in Yaroslav, or little Yaroslav, as the Gaevs amusedly call it. Ania is to be sent to Yaroslav to entreat help from her great aunt.

We first hear of the old aunt tucked away in Yaroslavl from Gaev:

GAEV: If a lot of cures are suggested for a disease, it means that the disease is incurable. I've been thinking and puzzling my brains, and I've thought of plenty of ways out, plenty - which means there aren't any. It would be a good thing if somebody left us some money, or if we married off our Anya to some very rich man, or if one of us went to Yaroslavl and tried our luck with the old aunt, the

Countess. You know she's very rich. . . . The Countess is very rich, but she doesn't like us . . .

And now again, in Act II:

GAEV: Our aunt in Yaroslavl promised to send us money but when and how much it will be we don't know.

LOPAKHIN: . . . A hundred thousand? Two hundred?

LIUBOV ANDRYEEVNA: Well, hardly. – Ten or twelve thousand, perhaps. We'll be thankful for that much.

The tedious brief brooding over the plot of the rich old countess in Yaroslavl is more or less concluded in Act IV, when the Gaevs are of all things giving a party on the day of the sale. Ranyevskaia is restlessly awaiting the return of Gaev from the auction:

LIUBOV ANDRYEEVNA: Still no Leonid. I can't understand what he's doing all this time in the town. In any case, everything must be over by now, either the estate's been sold or the auction never took place. Why must he keep us in ignorance so long?

VARIA: [*with that optimism that comes before the storm breaks*] Uncle bought it, dear Uncle, I'm sure he did. . . . Grandmamma sent us fifteen thousand roubles to buy the estate in her name, and transfer the mortgage to her. She's done it for Anya's sake. – God will help us, . . . Uncle will buy the estate.

LIUBOV ANDRYEEVNA: Grandmamma sent us fifteen thousand roubles to buy the estate in her name – she doesn't trust us, you see – but the money wouldn't even pay the interest. [*She covers her face with her hands.*] Today my fate is being decided, my fate . . . Why isn't Leonid back? I only want to know whether the estate's sold or not. Such a calamity seems so incredible that somehow I don't even know what to think, I feel quite lost. Honestly, I feel I could shriek out loud this very moment. . . .

Ania comes running on in a state of excitement:

ANIA: A man in the kitchen was saying just now that the cherry orchard was sold today.
LIUBOV ANDRYEEVNA: Sold? Who to?
ANIA: He didn't say. He's gone.
LIUBOV ANDRYEEVNA: I feel as though I'm going to die. Yasha, go, and find out who bought it.

Almost immediately Ranyevskaia gets her answer.

LIUBOV ANDRYEEVNA: [*to Lopakhin who has by now returned*] Well, what happened? Was there an auction? Speak, tell me!
LOPAKHIN: [*fearing to betray his joy*] The auction was over by four o'clock. – We missed our train and had to wait until half-past nine. . . . My head's going round.

Gaev comes in. Typically, in his right hand he has some delicacies in little packages, with his left he wipes away his tears. Ranyevskaia asks him, 'Well, Leonid? Tell me quickly, for God's sake!' Gaev makes no answer – his silence is answer enough. Instead he says to Feers, who has appeared at his elbow: 'Here,' he indicates his parcels, 'take this – it's some anchovies and Kerch herrings. – I've had nothing to eat all day. – What I've been through! I'm dreadfully tired . . .'

LIUBOV ANDRYEEVNA: Has the cherry orchard been sold?
LOPAKHIN: It has.
LIUBOV ANDRYEEVNA: Who bought it?
LOPAKHIN: I did.

Varia unfastens the silver chatelaine at her waist and flings the keys on the floor at Lopakhin's feet. She hurries blindly from the room. Lopakhin is too befuddled to do more than stare at them.

This is the supreme moment of his life.

The 'little serf', son of a serf, grandson of a serf, has bought the cherry orchard where once his family was enslaved.

LOPAKHIN: Yes, I bought it . . . I don't feel quite clear in my head, I hardly know how to talk – [*He laughs though he is nearer to tears.*] When we got to the auction, Deriganov was there already. Of course, Leonid Andryeevich only had fifteen thousand roubles, and Deriganov at once bid thirty over and above the mortgage. I could see how things were going, so I muscled in and offered forty. He bid forty-five, I bid fifty-five. He kept on adding five thousand each time and I added ten thousand each time. Well, it finished at last – I bid ninety thousand over and above the mortgage, and I got the property. Yes, the cherry orchard's mine now! Mine! [*Laughs.*] My God! the cherry orchard's mine! Come on, tell me I'm drunk, tell me I'm out of my mind, say I've imagined all this. [*Stamps his foot.*] . . . If only my father and grandfather could rise from their graves and see everything that's happened – how their Yermolai, their much-beaten, half-literate Yermolai, the lad that used to run about with bare feet in the winter – how he's bought this estate, the most beautiful place on God's earth! Yes, I've bought the very estate where my father and grandfather were serfs, where they weren't even admitted to the kitchen . . . [*Picks up the keys, smiling tenderly.*] She threw these down because she wanted to show she's not mistress here any more. Well, never mind. [*The band is heard tuning up.*] Hi! you musicians, come on now, play something, I want some music! [*to the company*] Now then, all of you, just you wait and see Yermolai Lopakhin take an axe to the cherry orchard, just you see the trees come crashing down! We're going to build a whole lot of new villas, and our children and great-grandchildren are going to see a new living world growing up here. – Come on there, let's have some music! [*The band plays* – probably with more spirit than correctness – LIUBOV ANDRYEEVNA *has sunk into a chair and is crying bitterly. Lopakhin turns to her reproachfully.*] Why didn't you listen to me before . . . my poor, dear lady, you can't undo it now. Oh, if only we could be done with all this, if only we could alter this distorted unhappy life somehow!

The eternal longing for reform which runs, like the shimmer of shot silk, through Chekhov's plays strives to make itself heard, yet again.

At the end of this act, too, when the party is over we see Liubov Ranyevskaia through the loving eyes of her young daughter:

ANYA: . . . The cherry orchard's sold, it's quite true . . . but don't cry, Mamma, you still have your life ahead of you, you still have your dear, innocent heart. You must come away with me, darling, we must get away from here! We'll plant a new orchard, even more splendid than this one – and when you see it you'll understand everything, your heart will be filled with happiness, like the sun in the evening; and then you'll smile again, Mamma! Come with me, darling, do come!

But in the end, her purse replenished by the money the ancient countess has sent for the auction, Liubov heads for Paris.

LIUBOV ANDRYEEVNA: That telegram's from Paris. I get one every day. – Yesterday and today. That savage is ill again, and things are going badly with him. – He wants me to forgive him, implores me to return, and really, I do feel I ought to go to Paris and stay near him for a bit. [*To Trofimov.*] You're looking very stern, Pyetia, but what's to be done, my dear boy, what am I to do? He's ill, and lonely and unhappy, and who's there to take care of him, to prevent him from making a fool of himself, and give him his medicine at the proper time? And anyway, why should I hide it or keep quiet about it? I love him, of course I love him. I do, I do. – It's a millstone round my neck, and I'm going to the bottom with it – but I love him and I can't live without him . . .

One somehow has the feeling that the cherry trees hang between the two off-stage presences – the aged countess in Yaroslavl and the profligate lover in Paris.

When next we come upon Madame Ranyevskaia she is planning to marry off her adopted daughter Varia to the 'little peasant', Lopakhin. It is Act IV. We are back in the sitting-room that was once the old night nursery, but it has been dismantled and is full of a variety of trunks, skips and baggage of all kinds. The Gaevs are taking their departure from the family home, leaving it for ever.

The peasants, off-stage, have come with their farewells and we find that even the loss of the house and the cherry orchard has not acted as a brake on Madame Ranyevskaia's generosity:

GAEV: [*accusingly*] You gave them your purse, Liuba. You shouldn't have done that. You really shouldn't.

LIUBOV ANDRYEEVNA: I couldn't help myself, I couldn't help myself!

Madame Ranyevskaia is anxious about Feers, the ancient retainer, whose health has been failing, but Anya tells her the old man has been sent off to hospital. Yasha, of all people, the flashy young footman, has been put in charge of this:

> ANYA: Has Feers been taken to hospital?
>
> YASHA: I told them to take him this morning. He's gone, I think. ... I told Yegor this morning. Need you ask ten times?

Soon Madame Ranyevskaia comes to say goodbye to her old night nursery:

> LIUBOV ANDRYEEVNA: Goodbye, dear house, old grandfather house. Winter will pass, spring will come again, and then you won't be here any more, you'll be pulled down. How much these walls have seen ... I'm leaving with two worries on my mind. One is Feers – he's sick ... The other is Varia. She's been accustomed to getting up early and working, and now, without work, she's like a fish out of water. She's got so thin and pale, and she cries a lot, poor thing. [*She turns to Lopakhin*] ... Yermolai Aleksyeevich, I'd been hoping to get her married to you – and everything seemed to show that you meant to marry her, too. She loves you ... and I ... just don't know why you seem to keep away from each other. I don't understand it.

But we do. It is only too likely that Varia, with her nun-like character, always at the service of others, and Lopakhin, the 'little peasant', conscious that in marrying Varia he would be aspiring to a daughter of the Family Gaev, to whom his family were serfs, would scarcely dare to look each other in the eye, far less speak endearingly to each other.

Varia is a simple, domestically minded girl, old before her years, like Sonia in *Uncle Vanya*, religious, again like Sonia. She is Madame Ranyevskaia's 'adopted daughter' and, as was the custom in the Russia of those days, treated as a member of the family. Chekhov himself called her a nun, but exposed to the pressures of Russian family life as she was, she must have been a very stormy nun. I have only once seen Varia played with spirit and serenity, and that was when she was played by that admirable actress, Dorothy Tutin, just as only once of many, many times have I seen the perfect Liubov Ranyevskaia, and that was Lila Kedrova. It may be that every one of Chekhov's carefully observed, lovingly transcribed characters have players born to play them. Certainly the compilation of perfect casts for the handful of plays that changed the course of nineteenth-century drama makes a perfect fireside game.

By contrast, Anya, the youngest of the family and everyone's pet, is a honied, hopeful girl, quite unlike any other young girl in the great quartet of plays; for Nina, trembling on the brink of love in *The Seagull*, is already troubled and under stress. Her stepfather does not approve of the Family Trepliov (fortunately the playgoer is not asked to approve them – only to love them) and already she is coping with the pull between Konstantin, the dreamer, and Trigorin, the man of the world.

Sonia, in *Uncle Vanya*, aware of her own plainness, hopelessly in love with the wood demon, is born to sorrow as the sparks fly upwards, and Irena, in *The Three Sisters*, has so short a time for happiness and is borne along, like her sisters, on a barren dream of Moscow.

But Anya, seventeen, is mistress of a bubbling spring in which her love for her mother and for Trofimov, the eternal student, and her belief in the future, shine out from the waters:

ANYA: You'll come back soon, Mamma – quite soon, won't you? I shall study and pass my exam at the high school and then I'll work and help you. We'll read all sorts of books together, Mamma . . . won't we? We'll read during the long autumn evenings . . . and a new, wonderful world will open up before us . . . [*Dreamily*.] Mamma, come back.

LIUBOV ANDRYEEVNA: . . . Now we can start on our journey!

ANYA: [*joyfully*] Yes, our journey!

Not that they go there and then, for this is a tale of the *ancien régime*.

First Varia and Lopakhin have to take leave of one another: she comes in looking for an object that she supposes she must have stowed away in one of the trunks by mistake. Throughout the little scene with Lopakhin she appears as much concerned with the lost object as with him. It is a way of hiding her shyness.

LOPAKHIN: Where are you going to now, Varvara Milhailovna?

VARIA: [*apparently intent upon her search in the luggage*] I? To the Rogulins. I've agreed to look after the house for them . . . to be their housekeeper . . .

LOPAKHIN: That's at Yashnevo, isn't it? About seventy miles from here. So this is the end of life in this house.

VARIA: . . . Yes, life in this house has come to an end – there won't be any more.

LOPAKHIN: And I'm going to Harkov . . . On the next train . . . Do you remember, last year about this time it was snowing already, but now it's quite still and sunny. It's rather cold, though. About three degrees of frost.

VARIA: [*going on with her searching*] I haven't looked. Besides, our thermometer's broken. [We may depend upon it the thermometer in any one of Chekhov's households is bound to be broken.]

[*A voice is heard from outside the door: 'Yermolai Aleksyeevich!'*]

LOPAKHIN: [*as if he had long been expecting it*] Coming this moment! [*He goes out quickly, leaving Varia sitting on the floor laying her head on a bagful of clothes sobbing quietly.*]

Leonid Gaev, the man born to be uncle, lost in his dream of billiards and caramels is, like Colonel Vershinin in *The Three Sisters*, a member of what passed in the professional classes of the Russia of his day as 'the intelligentsia'; but, lacking Vershinin's vision, he is an 'intelligent' gone to seed, though not so far gone in seed as Uncle Vania. He addresses himself to the furniture:

GAEV: ... My venerable dear bookcase! I salute you! For more than a hundred years you have devoted yourself to the highest ideals of goodness and justice. For a hundred years you have never failed to fill us with an urge to useful work; several generations of our family have had their courage sustained and their faith in a better future fortified by your silent call; you have fostered in us the ideal of public good and social consciousness.

LIUBOV ANDRYEEVNA: You're just the same, Leonid.

GAEV: [*slightly embarrassed*] I pot into the corner pocket!

He allows his young niece Anya to scold him:

GAEV: My dear little girl! [*Kisses* ANIA's *face and hands.*] My dear child! [*Through tears.*] You're not just a niece to me, you're an angel, you're everything to me. Please believe me, believe ...

ANYA: I believe you, Uncle. Everyone loves you, respects you – but, dear Uncle, you oughtn't to talk, you ought to try to keep quiet ...

GAEV: Yes, yes! ... And the speech I made today in front of the bookcase – so foolish! And it was only after I'd finished that I realized it was foolish.

Throughout the play Feers, the ancient retainer, scolds and cautions him:

FEERS: [*brushing Gaev, admonishing him*] You've put on the wrong pair of trousers again! What am I to do with you? . . . [*reproachfully*] Leonid Andryeevich, aren't you ashamed of yourself? When are you going to bed?

GAEV: [*He takes the great decision.*] Presently, presently. You go away, Feers. I don't need your help.

He admits he is hopeless with money:

GAEV: I've been offered a job at the bank. Six thousand a year. Have you heard?

LIUBOV ANDRYEEVNA: Indeed I have! You'd better stay where you are. [*Enter Feers with overcoat.*]

FEERS: Will you please put it on, Sir, it's so chilly.

GAEV: [*puts on the overcoat*] You *are* a nuisance.

FEERS: Tut, tut! You went off this morning and never told me you were going. [*Looks him over.*]

Frequently Gaev responds to a serious question from out of his dream of billiards, though now, for instance, he is out in the forlorn graveyard and nowhere near a table.

LIUBOV ANDRYEEVNA: . . . I keep expecting something dreadful to happen – as if the house were going to fall down on us.

GAEV: I pot into the middle pocket.

But one feels that Chekhov held Gaev very dear to him; is he not given the most loaded speech in the whole play as the sky turns to bronze in the evening? – 'The sun's gone down, ladies and gentleman.' – and we who watch feel, or should feel, that he is saying farewell to himself, and to his kind and to Holy Russia. For me, at least, this softly spoken epitaph is the crux of the play.

Yepihodov, 'two and twenty misfortunes', the estate clerk, is not the only character who is misfortune-prone. Trofimov, too, the 'eternal student', formerly tutor to Liubov's little son, seems particularly prone to disaster. The worst disaster of all befell himbefore the play opens, for Pietya was tutor to little Grisha, Madame Ranyevskaia's only son, and was out walking alone with him when the child drowned, six years ago. He and Anya are growing together, somewhere between understanding and romance, and it is from her that we first hear of him:

ANYA: We ought to warn Mamma that Pietya is here.

VARIA: I gave orders not to wake him.

ANYA: . . . Pietya Trofimov was Grisha's tutor, he might remind her.

But in spite of Varia's forethought and Anya's foreboding Trofimov appears on that night of homecoming, just as Liubov is luxuriating in her cherry orchard in the dawn light:

LIUBOV ANDRYEEVNA: What a wonderful orchard! Masses of white blossom, the blue sky.

TROFIMOV: [*appearing in a shabby student's uniform and spectacles*] Liubov Andryeevna! I'll just make my bow and go at once. [*Kisses her hand warmly.*] I was told to wait until the morning, but it was too much for my patience.

VARIA: This is Pietya Trofimov.

TROFIMOV: Pietya Trofimov, I used to be tutor to your Grisha. Have I really changed so much?

LIUBOV ANDRYEEVNA: My Grisha – my little boy – Grisha – my son.

VARIA: . . . It was God's will.

TROFIMOV: [*gently, with emotion*] Don't, don't . . .

LIUBOV ANDRYEEVNA: [*quietly weeping*] Why have you aged so? . . . In those days you were quite a boy, a nice young student, and now your hair is thin, you wear glasses. – Are you still a student?

TROFIMOV: Expect I shall be a student to the end of my days.

LIUBOV ANDRYEEVNA: [*wearily*] Well, go to bed now.

In the one-time graveyard of Act II we come upon Anya and Trofimov alone on the stage.

TROFIMOV: Varia's afraid – afraid we might suddenly fall in love with each other – so she follows us about all day long. She's so narrow-minded, she can't grasp that we are above falling in love . . . Let's march on irresistibly towards that bright star over there, shining in the distance! Forward!

ANYA: What have you done to me. Pictya? Why is it that I don't love the cherry orchard as I used to? I used to love it so dearly, it seemed to me that there wasn't a better place in all the world than our orchard.

TROFIMOV: The whole of Russia is our orchard. The earth is great and beautiful and there are many, many wonderful places on it. [*A pause.*] Just think, Anya: your grandfather and all your forefathers were serf owners – they owned living souls. Don't you see human beings gazing at you from every cherry tree in your orchard, from every leaf and every tree-trunk, don't you hear voices? – They owned living souls – and it has perverted you all, those who came before you, and you who are living now, so that your mother, your uncle and even you yourself no longer realize that you're living in debt, at other people's expense, at the expense of people you don't admit further than the kitchen. We are at least two hundred years behind the times; we still have no real background, no clear attitude to our past, we just philosophize and complain of depression, or drink vodka. Yet it's perfectly clear that to begin to live in the present, we must first atone for it by suffering, by extraordinary, unceasing exertion. You must understand this, Anya.

To understand that is to go a long way towards understanding

Chekhov, for Trofimov's whole speech resounds with his closely reasoned philosophy.

> TROFIMOV: You must believe me, Anya, you must. .... My soul is always. Every moment of the day and night, full of inexplicable forebodings, I have a foreboding of happiness . . .

Surely only in Chekhov could you find a person with a '*foreboding*' of happiness, or so I thought until one afternoon during a rainy break in the television transmission of tennis at Wimbledon one grey and brooding day, I heard a BBC commentator saying: 'I apprehend the sun will soon break through.'

> TROFIMOV: . . . The moon is rising. There it is – happiness – it's coming nearer and nearer, I seem to hear its footsteps. And if we don't see it, if we don't know when it comes, what does it matter? Other people will see it!

Yes, there is much of Chekhov himself in his eternal student.

It need not come upon us as a surprise to find that Trofimov, with his gaze so fervently upon the distant stars, is accident-prone on earth. In Act III, in the middle of the party, he remarks to Madame Ranyevskaia with considerable smugness that he and Anya are above love:

> LIUBOV ANDRYEEVNA: . . . You're able to solve all your problems in a resolute way but . . . isn't that because you're young, because you're not old enough to have suffered on account of your problems. . . . I would willingly let Anya marry you, honestly I would, but my dear boy, you must study, you must finish your course. You don't do anything, Fate seems to drive you from one place to another . . . And you should do something about your beard, make it grow somehow. – You are a funny boy!

Soon, though, she rounds on Trofimov:

> LIUBOV ANDRYEEVNA: You ought to be a man, at your age, you ought to understand people who are in love. And you ought to be able to love – to fall in love! [*Angrily.*] Yes, yes! And you're not 'pure', but you just make a fad of purity, you're a ridiculous crank, a freak.
> TROFIMOV: [*horrified*] What is she saying?
> LIUBOV ANDRYEEVNA: [*mimicking*] 'I'm above love!' . . . Not to have a mistress at your age!
> TROFIMOV: . . . I can't, I'm going. – [*Goes out, but returns at once.*] Everything's finished between us! [*He goes. There is a sound of someone running quickly downstairs, then falling suddenly with a crash. Anya and Varia scream, but laughter, too, is heard at once*]
> LIUBOV ANDRYEEVNA: What's happened?
> ANYA: [*laughing*] Pietya's fallen downstairs. [*Runs out.*]

Again, in the last act, when Varia searches among the trunks for galoshes, it is Trofimov who has lost them – it had to happen to him!

> VARIA: [*at length*] Pietya, here they are, your galoshes . . . And how dirty and worn-out they are!
> TROFIMOV: [*puts them on*] Come along, ladies and gentlemen!
> GAEV: [*afraid of weeping*] The train, the station. – In off into the middle pocket.
> ANYA: [*gaily*] Good-bye, old house! Good-bye, old life!

The peripheral characters in *The Cherry Orchard* are, like most of the peripheral people in Chekhov's plays, of interest in their own rights.

Take, for instance, Charlotta. In an age when most Russian families of any pretensions engaged an English *Miss* or a French

Mademoiselle Chérie (French being the language spoken in the home among the professional and upper classes), Madame Ranyevskaia's headlong household seems to have taken into its schoolroom a waif from a travelling circus who lingered on as the young ladies' chaperone, their Mamma being so much from home. We gather her thoughts on her early surroundings at the beginning of the second scene before an ancient shrine, long abandoned and, like the family she serves, fallen out of the perpendicular. Charlotta wears 'a man's old peaked cap; she has taken a shot-gun off her shoulder and is adjusting a buckle on the strap'.

> CHARLOTTA: [*thoughtfully*] I don't know how old I am. I haven't got a proper identity card . . . and I keep on imagining I'm still quite young. When I was little, my father and mother used to tour the fairs and give performances [Petrushka! Thou shoulds't be living at this hour!] – very good ones, they were, too. And I used to jump the *salto-mortale* and do all sorts of other tricks. When Papa and Mamma died, a German lady took me into her house and began to give me lessons. So then I grew up and became a governess. But where I come from and who I am, I don't know. Who my parents were – perhaps they weren't properly married – I don't know. [*She takes a cucumber from her pocket and begins to eat it.*] I don't know anything. [*a pause – no one is attending*] I'm longing to talk to someone, but there isn't anyone. I haven't anyone . . . who I am, what I exist for, nobody knows [*Goes out leisurely.*]

Charlotta gives the impression of striding through the play. She goes through her tricks at the party, and in the last act, when the stage is awash with luggage (one production I have seen even included a tin hip-bath), she even strives to make the sober household laugh:

> CHARLOTTA: [*Picks up a bundle that looks like a baby in swaddling clothes.*] Bye-bye, little baby. [*A sound like a baby crying is heard.*] Be quiet, my sweet, be a good little boy. [*The crying continues.*] My heart goes out to you, baby! [*Throws the bundle down.*]

A strange English *Miss* or possibly German *Fräulein*.

> ANIA: [*who has just returned from her trip to bring her mother back from Paris for the auction of the cherry orchard*] I left just before Easter: it was cold then. Charlotta never stopped talking, never left off doing her silly conjuring tricks, all the way. Why did you make me take Charlotta?
> VARIA: But how could you go alone, darling? At seventeen!

If in nothing else, the family is rich in characters.

Take Pishchik, a neighbouring landlord and hanger-on, for ever trying to borrow money but, what is more rare in borrowers, when money comes his way, paying it back. Pishchik offers good advice but a bad – and very funny – example to Liubov Ranyevskaia, who has been complaining of a headache:

> PISHCHIK: Don't take medicines, my dear – they don't do you any good – or harm either. Let me have them. [*Takes the box from her and pours the pills into the palm of his hand, blows on them, puts them all into his mouth and takes a drink of kvass.*] There!
> LIUBOV ANDRYEEVNA: [*alarmed*] But you're mad!
> PISHCHIK: [*proudly*] I've taken all the pills.
> LOPAKHIN: What a digestion! [*All laugh.*]

Save for falling suddenly asleep, Pishchik suffers no ill-effects. Now had it been two-and-twenty-misfortunes Yepihodov: 'Every day something or other unpleasant happens to me. But I don't complain; I'm accustomed to it, I even laugh at it.' But back to Pishchik, who wakes up from a nap – no doubt pill-induced – and says to Madame Ranyevskaia as he blinks open his eyes:

> PISHCHIK: . . . Incidentally, my dear, will you lend me two hundred and forty roubles? I've got to pay the interest on the mortgage tomorrow.
>
> LIUBOV ANDRYEEVNA: We haven't got it, we really haven't!
>
> PISHCHIK: It'll turn up. [*Laughs.*] I never lose hope. Sometimes I think everything's lost, I'm ruined, and then – lo and behold! – a railway line is built through my land, and they pay me for it! Something or other is sure to happen, tomorrow, if not today. Perhaps Dashenka (his daughter) will win two hundred thousand roubles. She's got a lottery ticket.

As with so many of the domestics met in Chekhov, the three in *The Cherry Orchard* repay a closer examination: Dooniasha, Yasha and particularly Feers, who speaks for the old order.

Dooniasha is what would have approximated to the upstairs *bonne à tout faire*. She does all the upstairs work with Varia and acts as maid to Madame Ranyevskaia and the young ladies. Dooniasha copies the family as closely as she can:

> DOONIASHA: My hands are trembling. I feel as if I'm going to faint.
>
> LOPAKHIN: You're too refined and sensitive, Dooniasha. You dress yourself up like a lady, and you do your hair like one, too. That won't do, you know. You must remember your place . . . I think I can hear them coming.
>
> DOONIASHA: Coming! – Oh, dear! I don't know what's the matter with me – I feel cold all over . . . [*agitated*] . . . I'm going to faint. – Oh, I'm fainting!

And so, at the opening of the play, we see into the pretensions of this upper servant. Earlier she has told Lopakhin that

Yepidohov has asked her to marry him. But 'two-and-twenty misfortunes' runs true to form, for Dooniasha dismisses him from the conversation with: 'I'm sure I don't know! He's a harmless fellow.' After a little more to that effect it is clear to us, too, that when Yasha, the flashy young houseman Madame Ranyevskaia took with her to Paris, appears on the scene Yepihodov will not have a look-in until he departs:

> YASHA: [*crossing the stage, in an affectedly genteel voice*] May I go through here?
>
> DOONIASHA: I can hardly recognize you, Yasha. You've changed so abroad.
>
> YASHA: Hm! And who are you?
>
> DOONIASHA: When you left here, I was no bigger than this. – [*Shows her height from the floor with her hand.*] I'm Dooniasha, Fiodor Kosoyedov's daughter. You can't remember!
>
> YASHA: Quite a little peach! [*Looks round, puts his arms round her; she cries out and drops a saucer.* YASHA *goes out quickly.*]

And later in Act II, in the abandoned graveyard which appears to act to the household Gaev as a kind of village green, Charlotta and the three servants are sharing the evening's respite. Yepihodov, 'two-and-twenty misfortunes', the estate bookkeeper, is in love with, but scorned by, Dooniasha, who is in love with but, ultimately, scorned by the lordly Yasha, personal manservant to Madame Ranyevskaia:

> YEPIHODOV: ... how pleasant it is to play the mandoline!
>
> DOONIASHA: [*scornfully*] That's a guitar not a mandoline.
>
> YEPIHODOV: [*reproachfully*] To a man that's crazy with love this is a mandoline. [*Sings quietly.*] 'If only my heart might be warmed by the ardour of love requited.'

Soon we are to see Yepihodov through his own eyes:

YEPIHODOV: I'm a cultured sort of fellow. I read all sorts of extraordinary books you know, but somehow I can't seem to make out ... to live or to shoot myself... [*proudly*] All the same, I always carry a revolver on me. Here it is ... [*pride ebbs*] I feel I simply must explain that Fate ... treats me absolutely without mercy, just like a storm treats a small ship ... Supposing I'm wrong for instance, then why should I wake up this morning and suddenly see a simply colossal spider sitting on my chest? Or supposing I pick up a jug of kvass, there's sure to be something frightful inside it, such as a cockroach ...

When Yepihodov is sent off on an errand by Dooniasha, to be rid of him, Yasha exclaims, 'two-and-twenty misfortunes'! He's a stupid fellow, between you and me.

Now we see Dooniasha through her own eyes:

DOONIASHA: I hope to God he won't shoot himself. [*Pause.*] I've got sort of anxious, worrying all the time. I came to live here with the Master and Mistress when I was still a little girl you see. Now I've got out of the way of living a simple life, and my hands are as white – as white as a young lady's. I've grown sensitive and delicate just as if I was one of the nobility; I'm afraid of everything. – Just afraid. If you deceive me, Yasha, I don't know what will happen to my nerves.

YASHA: [*kisses her*] Little peach! Mind you, a girl ought to keep herself in hand, you know. Personally I dislike it more than anything if a girl doesn't behave herself.

DOONIASHA: I love you so much, so much. You're educated, you can reason about everything.

YASHA: [*yawns*] Y-yes. – To my way of thinking, it's like this: if a girl loves somebody, it means she's immoral. [*Pause.*] It's nice to smoke a cigar in the open air. – [*Listens.*] Someone's coming this way. Our ladies and gentlemen. – Go home now, as if you'd been down to the river bathing; go by this path, or you'll meet them, and they might think I've been keeping company with you. I couldn't stand that.

Old Feers, the ancient retainer, is a servant of a quite different order. He looks after Leonid Gaev in his doddering way, like a long-handed-down nanny. It is clear that in his eyes Gaev is still a thoughtless youth, dangerously haphazard about his health. In Feers we have an example of the old order that fadeth not. He is the one character who never strives to pierce the veil that shrouds the future. Obviously he would have no time for the supercilious Yasha, nor Yasha for him; and indeed Yasha is inadvertently, at the close of the play, responsible for his death. For the family departs, each to their destination, the first of the cherry trees is felled – we hear the blows of the axe – and the house is locked up until the following spring, when it is to be pulled down. The ailing Feers, whom Yasha had been detailed to send off to hospital, is left alone and locked in.

> FEERS: They've gone. – They forgot about me. Never mind. – I'll sit here for a bit. I don't suppose Leonid Andryeevich put on his fur coat, I expect he's gone in his light one ... These youngsters! My life's gone as if I'd never lived. – I'll lie down a bit. [*Addressing himself.*] You haven't got any strength left, nothing's left, nothing – Oh, you – you're daft! [*Lies motionless.*] [*A distant sound is heard, coming as if out of the sky, like the sound of a string snapping, slowly and sadly dying away. Silence ensues, broken only by the sound of an axe striking a tree in the orchard far away.*]

It is the end of an era. Nothing is here for tears; yet everything. Chekhov's own words come back to us: 'It has turned out not a drama but a comedy, in places almost a farce.' The most gentle, most affectionate, most reflective of farces, then.

Yes, Chekhov had a magic touch with a minor part, just as he had with a major part. He looked about him. He listened. He missed no point or indication, and to everything he saw and heard he extended his understanding, his forgiveness, and his great heart.

Bibliography

Tchekoff, Anton, *Plays,* second series, trsl. Julius West (London 1920)

Tchehov, Anton, *The Cherry Orchard and Other Plays,* trsl. Constance Garnett, (London 1935)

Tchekhov, Anton, *Plays and Stories,* trsl. S. S. Koteliansky (London 1937)

Chekhov Anton, *Plays,* trsl. Elisaveta Fen (Harmondsworth 1959)

Chekhov, Anton, *Platonov,* trsl. Dmitri Makaroff (London 1961)

The Selected Letters of Anton Chekhov, ed. Lillian Hellman, trsl. Sidonie Lederer (London 1955)

Letters of Anton Chekhov, ed. Avrahm Yarmolinsky (New York 1973)

Letters of Anton Chekhov, ed. Simon Karlinsky, trsl. Michael Henry Hein (London, New York 1973)

Baring, Maurice, *Landmarks in Russian Literature* (London 1960)

BIBLIOGRAPHY

Laffitte, Sophie, *Tchekhov par lui-même* (Paris 1955)
Stanislavski, Constantin, *My Life in Art* (Harmondsworth 1967)
Styan, J. L. *Chekhov in Performance* (Cambridge 1971)
Tolstoy, L. *What is Art?* , trsl. Aylmer Maude (London 1930)
Gerhardi, William, *Anton Chekhov: A Critical Study* (London 1923)